LOST
AND
FOUND
IN
ALASKA

*A True Story of Survival and Miracles on
Kodiak Island...and Elsewhere*

D1453161

BRUCE LACHANCE
WITH MICHAEL A. MILARDO

outskirts
press

For my mother and father, who taught me that morals, hard work, and love are the meaning of life; and, as always, for my children and grandchildren- with all my love.

Slogan
Unto thine ownself be true- just for today.

TABLE OF CONTENTS

Introduction   I

Part One: Teachers and Heroes, Predators and Prey   1

Part Two: Lost and Found   39

Part Three: Lost Again   109

Part Four: God Moments and Miracles   127

Final Thoughts   142

About the Book   145

About the Author   146

INTRODUCTION

IN 1964, ELEVEN days before my twenty-first birthday, while serving in the United States Navy in Alaska, I experienced an adventure that most people would have found not only terrifying, but impossible to survive. To this day, however – I am now seventy-five years old – I thank God, my Higher Power, for everything I experienced while lost in the wilderness on Kodiak Island. Above all, I will always be immensely grateful for the countless solitary moments I spent soaked, cold, and losing weight – more than three pounds a day – not because they reinforced the already profound belief I had in myself, but because of how they would affect me much later in my life. As difficult as it may be to believe, while lost, I was never truly afraid. I *knew* I would survive. That self-confidence had been instilled in me not by a belief in a Higher Power – God was a mere "acquaintance" of mine at the time – but rather by the people in my life, especially my father, Joseph Ambrose LaChance, a navy veteran. And my hero. Only much later in life would I realize that losing my direction as a young man in Alaska's northern wilderness would pave the way to my experiencing the joy and beauty of truly finding myself, by one day acknowledging that all my self-confidence was of limited value and substance. Nothing but a fragile illusion. A delusion. Because thirty years after finding myself lost in Alaska, I would discover myself lost in the most terrifying wilderness of all. A kind of black hole. One void of light and hope but inundated with misery and pain. One without trust in one's self. Because there is no self. It has been lost. Shattered. True terror and slow death in small and big bottles, any kind of bottle or can, twenty-four hours a day, seven days a week, holidays especially. The addiction of alcohol. A wasteland far more deadly to me, and anyone else, than Alaska's wilds. Because at least there, even if lost and alone, one can find beauty and solace, belief and hope in the challenge and desire to survive.

Over the fifty-five years that have passed since those ten days spent wandering alone in the wilderness on Kodiak Island, I have lost and found myself numerous times, as we all do as part of the human experience, particularly us addicts on our rocky road to recovery, at least those of us who survive that journey. By admitting that we cannot travel it alone, no matter how much "self-confidence" we have. And by admitting we need help, and daring to ask for it, both from God and our fellow humans. Especially when all seems lost- those terrifying times of doubt, failure, self-condemnation, and fear that seem so overwhelming, so deadly, especially, perhaps, for us addicts. Because there is no Higher Power. There is no hope. There is no self. There is only the next high. The next drink. The denial that we have a problem. The lying to ourselves and others. And all the shame that goes with it. All the terrible, life-sucking shame. Until the next drink numbs you to it.

To this day, I remain awed by the fury and untamed beauty of the Alaskan wilderness. They represent the Creator's power and beauty. I realize now that I was never actually alone for those ten days I spent lost – a record amount of time for anyone who has survived being lost on Kodiak Island. In retrospect, I know my Higher Power who, as I have said, I never truly acknowledged during my adventure, even though I prayed to Him, only to abandon Him later, along with the Rosary beads I used to pray with – God figuratively tossed into a dumpster, the beads literally – accompanied me every step of the way in the wet and cold – guiding me back to civilization, at least as we define it, whispering in my brain which way to go. Not to track and kill a giant Kodiak bear, its meat going to the indigenous people, as was my original goal, but to find myself. Who I am. And Life's meaning.

As a recovering alcoholic, it has taken me twenty-five years of self-examination to realize that my time spent lost and "alone" in Alaska represented the birth of a lifesaving change in me, one that has made me who I am today: a kind, humble, *wise* man – I hope! – who has learned to accept Life's hardships as the path to peace. *If* I open my heart and arms to others and embrace their and His help, my ego, along with those of countless others, left behind at Life's door. In other words, a man still susceptible to foolish pride, but able to recognize it when I am. When those occasions occur, I feel angry, disappointed, and I chastise myself- because I have come to know and love who I truly am. Not in a selfish, egotistical, *deluded* way, but in a nurturing, self-caring way, the path to becoming a better person in a world that is *not* all about me, as my Higher Power began teaching me the instant I realized I was lost- not in Alaska, but in my addiction, and that I needed help. And the courage to ask for it. Until that moment of recognition arrived, and all throughout my Alaskan adventure, I had felt infallible, the very thought of asking or needing help an admission of failure. Defeat. But only God and Nature – they are really one and the same – are infallible. Eternal. And neither I nor anyone else can survive without their guidance and example- the lessons they and our fellow creatures offer us on how to live. In other words, they offer us the meaning of Life itself- if we seek to know their answers and offer our love in return. As I especially observed while lost on Kodiak Island, creatures we consider "beneath" us seem to have no problem living in harmony not only with this world, but with life and death. Only we humans seem to live at odds with ourselves and the world, and so we make this life and this planet contentious places, fraught with fear and danger. We seek salvation and in doing so, we tend to find and lose ourselves. Again. And again. And again. As we search long and hard, often despairingly, for a gift that will be granted- if we surrender ourselves to our Higher Power– "the serenity to accept the things we cannot change, courage to change the things we can, and the wisdom to know the difference." It is the struggle we must all endure in pursuing how to live and who we are, and not the mere pursuit of a twelve-hundred-pound Kodiak bear, somewhere in Alaska.

I hope you will now allow me to tell you all about my experience of getting lost and found fifty-five years ago on Kodiak Island, and later in my life. Again. And again. And again. Until, with my Higher Power's help, and that of the angels in this world, I finally found my way and realized that miracles exist not only in the world around us, but within ourselves. Within our souls. If we choose to open our eyes, hearts, and minds to them, and abandon our egos and fears. That's what salvation demanded from me, and perhaps demands from us all. And so, over many years, I have come to realize that not only were the ten days I spent lost in Alaska a lifesaver for me, they were also nothing less than a miracle. Looking back, until I wandered away from humanity as a naïve young man and then lost my way in alcohol as an equally naïve older man, I had never believed in miracles. But I do now. And I always will. I think by the time I finish telling you my story, you will understand why. And that as you continue your journey, possibly finding and losing yourself again and again, just like me, perhaps hitting rock bottom, just like me, you can take comfort in your blessings and who you are: another of Life's countless precious miracles, the same as all of God's creatures. The same as Life.

Best regards,
Bruce LaChance
January 1, 2020

PART ONE
TEACHERS AND HEROES,
PREDATORS AND PREY

1.

ON SEPTEMBER 19, 1961, at the age of seventeen, following in my father's footsteps, I enlisted in the United States Navy. Due to my age, I entered the navy on what was called a "minority tour"- three years of active duty, followed by three years of inactive service. Radioman school didn't start until six months after boot camp, so in the interim, I was assigned sea duty aboard the USS Sierra. I discovered, however, that the USS Tidewater was heading to the Mediterranean for a six-month cruise, and I was able to get my duty transferred. For the first time in my life, I began to explore the world far beyond my quaint, little hometown of Avon, Connecticut, population about 2,200.

Upon returning to port in Norfolk, Virginia and then in Banebridge, Maryland, I began radioman school and did well enough to get chosen in February of 1963 to serve on the admiral's staff on Kodiak Island, on Alaska's northern sea frontier. For me, it was a dream come true. Ever since I was a boy I had loved to hunt. And now I dreamed of one day hunting a Kodiak bear. That day and that dream would arrive soon enough, but in the form of a nightmare- for most people. One that makes you sit up and scream.

Growing up, I was a good kid, blessed to enjoy all the benefits that a solid, hard-working, blue-collar family could possibly provide. Very early on in my life, my mother and father began to instill a strong work ethic in me, one that their parents, along with bitter lessons learned from the Great Depression, had instilled in them. At eight years old, with my parents' encouragement, I began a paper route delivering the *Hartford Times* in Avon, a Hartford suburb. Through my paper route, along with church activities and my parents, I got to know many people in town and became friends with most of them. Eventually, however, my struggles with learning in school, due largely to my self-diagnosed dyslexia – I was never formally diagnosed – coupled with chronic hearing problems – I had many severe earaches as a child – severely hampered my cognitive progress. These problems would continue to plague me, even at age twenty, as I struggled to learn what I needed to become a navy radioman. But of the many values my parents had instilled in me by then, perhaps foremost among them was what my father had taught me to believe- that I could accomplish anything, overcome any obstacle, if I set my heart and mind to it. In other words, if I *believed* in myself. Much later in my life, however, I would realize that that belief could be a two-headed serpent. Sure, it helped me believe in myself and overcome disabilities to accomplish my goals. But it could also blind me with arrogance. Drinking? No way will it get the better of me. I've got it all under control. I can stop whenever I want. I don't need any help. Yeah, that's what we all tell ourselves. Until some of us hit rock bottom – for the final time – and look up and see the light. Or die.

My father, of course, could never realize the negative possibilities of his lessons in self-confidence. But he was a good man, and as I grew up, we did a lot together. He was my hero. Joseph A. LaChance had served in the navy as a snipe, an engine man, aboard the USS Chicago, and was discharged shortly before the start of World War II. Upon leaving the service, my mother and father married, with my sister arriving in this world about two years before me. After the war had started, while my dad was working servicing the cooling systems of jet engines at Pratt & Whitney Aircraft in East Hartford, Connecticut, and making very good pay at that, he received a letter from the commanding officer on the USS Chicago inviting him to return as a Chief Petty Officer aboard the ship. He would also be serving with many of the same crewmen as before, some of them good friends. My father was tempted, all but agreeing to return to active duty, when my mother talked him out of it. No way, she insisted, with one child already and, hopefully, someday another, could he leave Pratt & Whitney. My father agreed. He was lucky he did. After surviving a midget submarine attack at Sydney Harbour and serving in battle at the Coral Sea and Savo Island in 1942, the USS Chicago was sunk by Japanese aerial torpedoes in the Battle of Rennell Island, in the Solomon Islands, on January 30, 1943. As a result, that same day, my father vowed to always listen to my mother. And that was why she always had the last word in any of their future arguments, including the one over whether or not I should own a gun.

As I have said, my dad was my hero. He could fix anything, and even when I was as young as three or four, he always welcomed my help. Or seemed to. When I was five, I "helped" him repair the brakes on a '41 Chevy by sitting in the driver's seat and pumping the brake pedal to bleed fluid from the line. I pumped a bit too hard and brake fluid flew into my father's eyes. I cried because I thought I had done something terrible, that it was all my fault. And that I had disappointed my father. But my dad, always cool, calm, confident, a soft-spoken gentleman in the true sense of the word, merely explained that because of the way he was trying to bleed the brakes, with me pumping them, what had happened was really his fault, not mine. It was one of my dad's many lessons in kindness and patience that I would never forget, except at times later in life, when alcohol had me under its spell, and I was convinced I was the center of the universe, in need of no one's help. Kindness? I could be kind to others, but not myself. I was losing myself.

In 1950, my dad helped my Uncle George, my mother's brother, build his home. Like my father, Uncle George was one of my heroes while I was growing up. He was a glazier for Local 1339 out of Hartford and worked with all types of glass, while doing storefront work, home window repairs, and window installation in skyscrapers. One of Uncle George's favorite jokes came whenever someone asked him, "What does a glazier do? What do you glaze?" George's smiling, mischievous response was always the same: "I glaze donuts." It made me smile, too, despite some of the things that I had come to realize about Uncle George.

As my father helped Uncle George build his house, the two men allowed me to help them in any way a seven-year-old possibly could. As I have stated already, my father lived to a high moral code of conduct that helped instill an immense amount of confidence in me and everything I did. I will always remember him telling me, "If you need to use four-letter words as adjectives, it only shows a lack of education and knowledge on your part." But my father had no interest in hunting. I did. And so did my Uncle George. Gladly, when we weren't working on his house, Uncle George would take me fishing or hunting, and teach me all he knew about both. Like my father, he was an excellent teacher. And though he was a bigot, ironically, he often championed the underdog – in this case, my friends and me – with a passion. For that reason, and because Uncle George shared his immense knowledge of hunting and fishing with me, I regarded him as a hero, despite his bigotry. He talked to me and treated me as his equal. I saw both sides of Uncle George, the one I admired and sought to emulate, and the one I did not.

On Christmas morning, 1955, when I was twelve, in a manner much like Ralphie's in the movie, *A Christmas Story*, my wish for my first gun finally materialized. As always, along with our relatives – about a dozen cousins and their parents – we had spent Christmas Eve at Gramma and Grampa Carter's home- my mother's parents. Adhering to tradition, the festivities began around eight in the evening with all us kids playing and carousing upstairs and downstairs, while the adults gathered in the kitchen to enjoy their adult beverages – and lots of them – leaving me to wonder what it was about alcohol that made them think it tasted so good, and made them laugh so much. After all, it smelled terrible. Someday, I decided, I would find out. Oh, how I would find out...

Around ten on Christmas Eve, amid boisterous caroling, we all gathered around my grandparents' tree to open gifts, most of the adults still with drinks in hand. Once midnight approached, and all the singing, drinking, and laughter ended, and final well-wishes had been said, off to mass I went with my sister Sandy and our parents. In church, my curious eyes searching all around, I noticed more than one man sitting, standing, or kneeling nearby with a rare roast beef-colored neck, face flushed, breath hot, smelling of alcohol, even from five or six feet away. And when it came time for everyone to kneel and pray, and those men wearily fell to their knees, I wondered what adults prayed for. God's help? For Him to watch over them and their families? Peace in their crazy adult world? Personally, I prayed for a gun.

The following morning, as was our wont, my sister Sandy and I rose at the crack of dawn to open our gifts that, as if they had been placed beneath the tree not by our parents, but by the miracle of Christmas's own hands, waited for us amid a show of multi-colored lights and shimmering tinsel. The electrified, magical memories of a childhood Christmas - but still no sign of a gun. Perhaps, a not-so-magical Christmas, after all.

Later that Christmas morning, around nine, our mom and dad finally came downstairs to join Sandy and me. After opening their gifts – I no longer remember what they gave each other, or what Sandy and I gave them, too many years have passed – my mother asked what gifts I had gotten. After I told her – again, I don't remember what they were – she asked if I had received anything else. Perhaps, she heard the disappointment in my voice and saw it in my eyes when I answered, "No," and said nothing more.

My mother then asked, "Have you looked in the corner behind the tree?"

Looking toward the corner, squinting my eyes to see better, still seeing nothing, I shook my head and replied, "No."

"Well," said my mother, with what I perceived as a twinkle in her eye, "why don't you go and take a closer look?" Now both her eyes twinkled, as brightly as the lights on the tree, I thought. Quickly I headed for the secluded corner behind the tree, hoping to find a miracle in the shadows…

And I did! Much to my mother's delight, and my father's dismay – my mom, having come from a family of hunters, had favored my getting a gun, my father had opposed it – I took the Stevens 410/22 in my hands to examine, admire and worship, as if it were an idol. Or a longed-for miracle finally come true. One that would pale in comparison to those true miracles I would experience much later in life, but only when my face, unlike those of the men in church that midnight in 1955, was no longer flushed, my breath no longer fiery, my thoughts no longer scrambled- from my disease, the addiction of alcoholism.

As it turned out, the first animal I ever shot was not with my new Stevens 410/22, but with an old bow and arrow I had while out hunting alone one day in some woods near my home shortly after that Christmas. My prey had been a gray squirrel, but when I approached the tiny body, I saw that my arrow had only stunned and grazed it. To put it out of its misery, I stabbed the squirrel many times with the arrow. Though I begged it to die, it seemed to refuse. Tears welling, I felt sorry for the creature, its soft, dark eyes forever closed. But I was also scared that someone had seen what I had done- the repeated stabbing, as if I were crazed – and I would be in trouble. Big trouble. Quickly I buried my victim, its tiny heart no longer ticking. Then I went to tell Uncle George what I had done, but he was off somewhere else hunting, so I told Aunt Cecelia instead. Immediately, eyes alit, she told me to go get the squirrel and bring it to her- so she could add it to the game dinner she was planning to prepare that night.

Spirits lifted, I smiled and nearly exclaimed "Great!" out loud, the burden of guilt suddenly free from my heart and shoulders, now that I was a contributor. I had killed for a cause, a good cause- a delicious, wild-game meal that everyone would enjoy. I thanked the squirrel for that.

Saturday was hunting day, but first came Friday night and card games at Uncle George's. Several of the card players were his hunting partners, and they always discussed their plans for Saturday while playing poker or rummy. Then in the morning, they would gather at around 5:30 or 6:00 for breakfast before heading out to hunt. I would always arrive at the same time with my .22 and sit beneath the Sophia bush between my grandparents' house and Uncle George's and wait until the hunters had finished eating. No one even knew I was there. Finished eating, the hunters would then leave together in one of their cars. As I have said, because my father was no hunter, he never joined them. Once they had left, I would come out from beneath the Sophia bush to go off and hunt squirrels by myself in an area where I could safely fire my gun. On one of those occasions, when I was around fifteen, I ran into a hunter named Ray, and we became fast friends. And just as quickly, Ray became another mentor in my life. Upon introducing ourselves to one another, Ray immediately informed me that he was deaf but able to read lips. Despite his hearing impairment, however, Ray was an excellent communicator and teacher. Like Ray, I had hearing problems, mine due to my numerous earaches. What I initially learned from him, other than how to overcome a handicap, was to be patient- echoing my father's own lessons in kindness and patience. But from Ray I learned to be especially patient when struggling to overcome adversity. That lesson would serve me well for the rest of my life, especially just five years after meeting Ray, when I lost my way in the wilderness on Kodiak Island.

Though Ray was in my life only during that autumn in 1959, his memory remains vivid, even powerful. Ray and I both enjoyed hunting squirrels, which consisted mostly of just sitting, watching, and waiting, often for long periods of time. A lesson not only in patience and perseverance, but in turning a negative – in this case deafness – into a positive. To use a cliché, perhaps partially due to his inability to hear, Ray had eyes like a hawk. But foremost, he taught me strength of character and belief in oneself, again reinforcing what my father had already begun to instill in me. Our strategy, devised by Ray, was simple. We sat apart, out of each other's sight, totally silent, unless one of us fired a shot. Often when I shot a squirrel, I would only wound it, and I would have to quickly shoot it again. Usually, it required four or five shots for me to bag two squirrels. But Ray had a method that was unique- and productive. By waiting for two squirrels to come into the same line of fire, he could bag them both with just one shot. Four squirrels with just two shots? No problem for Ray- he had the eye and the aim to do it. And for me, it was yet another lesson- in creative thinking and ingenuity. Essences for survival, anywhere, especially in the wilderness.

After hunting, I always gave what squirrels I had bagged to Ray and, in return, he would take me to Luto's, a small restaurant on Route 44 in Canton, Connecticut, where he would treat me to one of Mr. Luto's delicious homecooked meals. And in doing so, serve up examples of what kind of man, as my father had already exemplified to me, I should learn to be- one who is kind and generous, and who treats others as he wants to be treated. How we all want to be treated. With respect and consideration. The essences of friendship. Peace and harmony.

Quickly the friendship Ray and I shared came to include Mr. Luto, as I realized one morning when Ray arrived late for yet another of our Saturday morning squirrel-hunting expeditions. Upon his arrival, I instantly perceived from his big grin and urgent motions that Ray was excited about something he had in the trunk of his car. He was frantic to show me what it was. When he opened the trunk, I saw a red fox he had shot and, momentarily, I lost my breath. Both of us now equally excited, rather than hunt squirrels, we immediately drove to the restaurant to show Mr. Luto Ray's "trophy" and share our excitement with him. Since Ray had shot the fox near a populated area in Avon, I liked to think that pet owners had been spared the grief of having their own animals killed, the predator's death justified, as is sometimes the case with human predators, those that have or would kill others. In the end, as I knew it would be, Mr. Luto's elation was equal to ours. That's how it is with friends, even if that friendship is for just one autumn. Leaves fall, trees turn barren, but memories of good times, like those I shared with Ray and Mr. Luto, are indelible. They are one of time's lessons.

As I have said about another of my heroes when I was growing up, I learned from my mother and father, and through my own perceptions, that my Uncle George was a bigot, a man I should never emulate in that regard. But I also could not stop liking him, at least that part of him that was not tainted with bigotry, the part of him that treated a young boy like me with kindness and respect, as if I were his equal- a fellow adult. Plus, he taught me all he knew about my two greatest loves at the time – hunting and fishing – and even Uncle George's lessons would later prove invaluable in my struggle to survive while lost on Kodiak Island. To reiterate, he was a complex man with many good qualities- and one bad one. His bigotry. Like all prejudices, his had been taught, the lessons learned rock-solid within him, part of his stubbornness. Arguing with a brick was easier than arguing with Uncle George. He was that hard-headed. But before saying anything more about him, let me say this: Being alone when lost has its benefits. All decisions are yours, and yours alone. You share no responsibility- for anything. Therefore, there are no arguments- unless you choose to doubt and argue with yourself.

At age sixteen, after I had gotten my first hunting license, Uncle George, with whom I hunted, also began taking me fishing with him.

Perhaps, those times were his foremost gift to me. Along with those occasions when he taught me to stick up for *certain* underdogs, like my neighborhood friends, when they were unjustly accused of committing certain "criminal" acts, like breaking a window, or trespassing on someone's property. Uncle George always acted as a mediator to resolve the issue, though, at times, perhaps a bit too vociferously, especially when he knew my friends were in the right, clearly innocent of any and all charges. Thus, I learned from one of the world's most stubborn men and his tunnel-vision-views of people and the world this renowned lesson: take what you need…and leave the rest. Uncle George's sister, my mother, Irene Carter LaChance, taught me the same lesson, time and again. Unlike my dad, on most occasions and with most people, my mom lacked patience as a virtue. Often, she had no patience, at all, the opposite of what would prove necessary to me years later, while lost in the Alaskan wilderness. But at least I recognized that flaw in her, both during my time on Kodiak Island when survival demanded patience, and much later, when I was not only lost, but drowning in alcohol. Recovery *demands* patience and self-care.

Sometimes, when I was a kid, my mother became so impatient with me that she slapped me. Like when she lost her temper because, for the life of me, I could not remember my spelling words. Dyslexia? My mom had no idea that was the cause of my learning disability. How could she? In the early 1950s, how could anyone? Along with her ill temper, my mother also held grudges. Despite her character "defects," however, and my frequent inability to relate to her because of her temper, I loved my mother. And despite my "shortcomings," she believed I was the best thing since mothers' milk, and the best thing that ever happened to her, with all due respect to my older sister, Sandra. My mother praised me to no end when I did something right. Like the time she went outside with my dad and forgot she had pork chops cooking on the stove. Realizing she had forgotten about them, seeing the smoke starting to rise, immediately I removed the pan from the burner and turned off the flame. When my mother returned inside and saw that I had "saved" both her and the chops, all was right between me and her and the world. As always, dinner would be delicious, and on time- thanks to Bruce.

Things between my mom and me would change in more positive ways as I got older, and she would do her best to show me that she loved me. Thinking of her years later, I realized that during my teen years, she was always there for me, like the time when I was fourteen and needed braces for my teeth. My mom, always the devoted mother and housewife, immediately went out and got a job outside our home to pay the $1,500 bill, a year's pay for her. And when I fell off the roof of the chicken coop in our backyard, she was the first to come to my aid, as was the case when I fell off my bike and landed on a broken Coca-Cola bottle. Due to the cuts I suffered on my right hand, I temporarily lost the use of three fingers. But my mother took good care of me and made sure no infections set in. Later, she showed her selflessness, love, and generosity in other ways. Through her jobs outside the house that added to my father's income, we were able to purchase a house trailer and a boat and spend summers at Connecticut's Hammonasset State Park. Though at times a tempestuous "piece of work," my mother, Irene LaChance, right up until the day she died, on Friday, October 13, 2006, was indeed a remarkable woman. Her lessons and examples, and the character traits she and my father instilled in me as a youngster, would one day contribute to my surviving Alaska's deadly wild. Thank God for my mother and father.

Clearly, while growing up, I had a passion for the outdoors. I still do. Hunting was supreme, but I also loved fishing, and with Uncle George's help, I quickly became very good at it. As fishermen and pals, we fished together from Uncle George's old aluminum boat. After casting my line, it was always my job to troll. Though not many of my teenaged friends enjoyed fishing, I fished whenever possible using my family's wooden rowboat- nearly every day during the summer, always alone. Gradually, I got to know nearly everyone who lived on the lake, and I was quick to say, "Hi!" Often, I stopped to help people with their chores and projects. I liked to think they knew they could depend on me, just as I and everyone else could depend on my father, that value of his having been thoroughly instilled in me. Everyone knew they needn't ask for my help. I was always quick to volunteer. Ironically, in retrospect, I had no problem asking other people if they needed help, but me ask for help? No way! I never needed help. Until much later in my life, when I finally had to admit to myself that I did. Or else, like all alcoholics, all addicts, I would die.

One day when I was out alone trolling on the lake, I passed the house of a man whose acquaintance I had made already. I'm still glad I did, because from that day on, though he was in my life for only one brief summer, we became fast friends. As with my Uncle George, Mr. Baril spoke respectfully to me, as if I were an adult. And soon I came to idolize him, our time together a treasure. That day I asked him if he would like to go fishing sometime. Instantly he replied, "Sure!" and we agreed to go one evening soon. Again, I'm glad we did- because I came to cherish not only Mr. Baril's companionship, but all he would teach me.

When the agreed upon evening arrived, at 5' 8" and well over two hundred pounds, Mr. Baril could barely squeeze himself into the back seat of my small boat. And though he always looked uncomfortable squashed into his seat, like me, Mr. Baril loved fishing. That first night out together, however, we caught nothing. The next evening, when we decided to fish from the dock in his backyard, was a different story- due to Mr. Baril's unique and imaginative fishing technique, and the contraption he had devised for it. At first, the apparatus baffled me, but soon I appreciated Mr. Baril's remarkable ingenuity, as any fisherman would. It consisted of two narrow, hollow aluminum tubes from a TV antenna, each about three and a half feet long, joined together to form a rod; two wooden thread spools placed one above the other at the end of about fifty feet of line, with two tiny bells attached near the top spool; a two-ounce weight at the end of the line; a hook with an eight-inch leader about a foot up from the weight; and a cork bobber about a foot up of from the hook. The other end of the line was anchored at the top spool to the front of his backyard dock, into which Mr. Baril had hammered two horseshoe nails.

Once everything had been prepared – actually, it was much simpler than it sounds – Mr. Baril, after instructing me to keep my feet still to prevent them from getting tangled, had me start removing all the line from the spools. Again, following his directions, I then placed all the line between my motionless feet, pulling on it until I got to the end, where the bobber, hook, and weight were attached. Finally, I baited the hook, and then grabbing the line above the bobber, I cast it out into the water. After pulling the slack from the line and feeling the pull of the two-ounce weight, I let go slightly until the bobber stopped moving; after which, as directed, I wedged the line between the top spool and the aluminum rod.

"Now Bruce, come have a seat next to me," said Mr. Baril, squeezing himself into a lawn chair near the edge of the water, and then cracking open a beer. As I sat, Mr. Baril, after sipping his beer and following it with a prolonged, "Ahhhhh…then crossed his legs and said, "When a fish bites, the bells ring. When they do, get up out of your chair, take the line between the tube and the spool, and wait till the fish takes the bait. And then hook him. Again, while you're doing that, don't move your feet because you'll get tangled and lose everything. When you pull in your catch, it'll be an eel or a bullhead. And then you start the process all over again…while just sitting here. No fuss, no muss." He sipped his beer again.

True to his word, as always, Mr. Baril's odd contraption worked. We spent many evenings together fishing from his yard, and soon I realized that here was yet another mentor and hero in my life, someone, as time would tell, I would never forget. Unlike a man I haven't mentioned yet, Mr. Baril's opposite, my Uncle Fred, another of my mother's brothers-in-law. A hunter, Uncle Fred had beagles and successfully competed in hunting trials with them. He particularly enjoyed hunting rabbits, and often went up to Maine to hunt bigger game. Despite knowing that I loved hunting, Uncle Fred never asked me to join him, making him another kind of man a boy never forgets. I resented Uncle Fred. Maybe I still do, which says a lot about the pain in our lives, especially the hurt we experience as infants and adolescents. It can haunt us forever. Now, for me, the best thing to do is recall these words from the Serenity Prayer: "…grant me the serenity to accept the things I cannot change, courage to change the things I can, and the wisdom to know the difference. Living one day at a time, enjoying one moment at a time, accepting hardship as the path to peace…" It works every time, if you give it a chance.

Back to Mr. Baril, and a few words and a final memory of him. One evening during our summer of friendship, Mr. Baril asked me if I had a kerosene lantern that we could use while fishing from his yard at night. I said I did, but that it was old and rusty and in need of repair. He said to bring it to him, anyway, which I did.

A few evenings later, when I returned to fish, he gave me what I thought was a brand-new lantern. Moments later, I realized he had refurbished my old one, painting the glass on one side black, the glass on the other side silver. Thus, when we sat facing the lantern while night fishing, the dark side never blinded us while the silver side illuminated the dock, along with our lines. More than fifty years later, I still have the lantern. How cool is that? And what a lucky kid I was to have so many friends and heroes, especially ones like Mr. Baril!

In June 1961, I became a member of the first graduating class from Avon High School. Upon graduating, I worked for a house painter for the summer. Since I was a terrible painter – too messy, too wasteful, too slow – I was assigned to paint the insides of closets, where my lack of talent was far less glaring. One day while the boss was away, the rest of us were painting the kitchen at the YWCA in Hartford. Like painting only house closets, as the "inside" guy, my job was to paint the inside of the ceiling's exhaust fan shaft- and nothing else. After turning off the fan, I climbed between the large blades into the shaft, only my feet remaining atop the ladder. Reaching as far as I could inside the shaft, I began to paint. Meanwhile, with no boss to supervise us, two other painters worked in the kitchen, adding a fresh coat of glossy white paint over the yellow-stained walls. A few hours later, after coffee break, I returned inside the shaft to finish my work. Immediately I realized I had forgotten to bring my paint bucket. So, I called to one of the other painters – Charlie – to pass it up to me.

"Come on back down and get it yourself!" bellowed Charlie. I imagined a big, shit-eating smile on his face, mischievous eyes twinkling behind his thick, horn rimmed glasses. Finally, he passed the bucket up to me. But not until he had painted my black work shoes white as I struggled to back out of the shaft and reach down for it. Round one to the wily vet over the naïve high school grad, and we all laughed.

Later in the day, nearly finished painting the shaft, working my way back towards the fan, as I did, I plotted my revenge. Prepared to descend the ladder, I called to Charlie to climb up and take my paint bucket. As soon as his face appeared atop the ladder, just as he reached to take my bucket, a big, shit-eating grin spread across *my* face…and I painted the lenses of Charlie's glasses. Thrilled with my revenge, laughing as Charlie grumbled and cursed, I scrambled down the ladder- only to find myself face to face with our boss, Billy Bonizelly, who was none too pleased, to say the least.

"It's bad enough that you can't paint worth shit!" he barked in my face. "But ya can't keep these other guys from working!"

Carefully examining Charlie's glasses, the lenses still coated white, I replied, "I think I did a fine job painting Charlie's glasses," which made even Billy laugh. Round two to the rookie.

A week later, my brief stint as possibly the world's worst painter ended abruptly, and my gateway to the future opened. I was working on a job in Avon, using an electric sander to remove old, chipped paint from the clapboards of a house. I was alone, the rest of the crew working at another job in West Hartford, when it began to rain around 2:00 p.m. Unable to continue working outside with the electric sander, I packed up everything and went home. Later, around 4:30, Billy showed up at my house and asked, "Why'd ya leave the job, Bruce?"

"Because it was raining, and I couldn't use the sander," I immediately responded, disbelief replacing irritation on Billy's face as his eyes darkened and he snapped, "That's bullshit! I was in Avon on the other side of the mountain at two o'clock, and it wasn't raining there."

Realizing I could never convince Billy that I was telling him the truth, though furious because he had accused me of lying, I decided to let things go as Billy quickly turned and left, shaking his head all the way to his truck.

The following day, ironically, while using the electric sander at the same job in Avon, suddenly it began to rain again. Because of what had happened the previous day, I kept working. Around two, Billy suddenly appeared. Over the course of the previous evening and that morning, my rage toward Billy had returned.

"What the hell are you doing?" he yelled, as if I were a moron. "Trying to kill yourself? Get down from there!"

Immediately I followed his order, climbed down the ladder, and put the sander and chord in his truck. Then, with fists clenched, I let Billy have it.

"Listen you bastard!" I nearly spat in his face, ignoring what my father had instilled – or had attempted to instill in me – about using foul language. "Yesterday I picked up and went home because it was raining. Today it rains, I stay and work, and you're giving me hell again. I hope it rains tomorrow, because if it does, I'm joining the navy."

Sure enough, it rained the next day and, true to my word, I drove to Hartford, where, following in my father's footsteps, I enlisted. Looking back, it was the best thing I could have ever done for myself.

It completely changed my views of the world, in ways I never could have imagined, as you will see. Because I was only seventeen, however, my parents had to sign a consent form. Though my dad was proud and pleased to do so, my mother's tight lips and dark eyes upon hearing the news instantly revealed her passionate disapproval of my decision.

But there was no going back. I spent all the following week trying to convince my mother, as mule headed as her brother George, that it was the best path in life for me, and that she should sign along with my father. For me, her signing would also symbolize that she approved of me and the decision I had made as a man. One week later, after having passed a test that determined the navy would provide technical school-ing for me, my father accompanied me back to Hartford. My mother did not. As it turned out, only my dad signed the consent form, which was good enough for both me and the navy. I could live with my moth-er's decision. After all, I was still the "best thing since breast milk." And now I was about to become a sailor and a radioman, about to go on the adventure of a lifetime.

2.

When I was around ten years old, I said to myself, "I'll never be able to drink when I get older because I'll become an alcoholic." That thought stayed with me throughout high school and into the service. Unlike my stalwart, self-disciplined father, three of his brothers were alcoholics, as were my mother's father and one of her brothers. So even at the age of ten, I had become aware of what an alcoholic is, and the devastating effects alcohol can have on some people's lives. That some people could control it, and some could not.

When I was around fifteen, I got drunk for the first time in my life. It happened while I was camping with my family at Hammonassett State Park in Madison, Connecticut. One day, two of my buddies showed up with a pint of whiskey. Around six that evening, we polished off the whiskey, each of us chugging down about a third of the bottle. To this day, I have no memory of what my friends and I did afterward, because besides getting drunk for the first time, I also experienced my first blackout. I came to only when I realized that one of my friends' mothers was holding my head under an outdoor water spigot on the campgrounds. Eventually, I was able to recall crawling into my tent and plopping down on my cot, my mom and dad asleep in our camper. Eyeballs rolling in my skull, the world tilting and whirling around me, I was finally able to brace one foot firmly to the ground to keep my cot from spinning and eased myself down. That was the only time I ever got drunk, until many years later, when a miracle in the form of a set of Rosary beads that I had carried with me while lost on Kodiak Island, and then discarded, suddenly reappeared in my life, paving the way to what would be, for me, my sole hope for salvation by then: my 12-Step Program. Much more about those beads and miracles, later.

On September 19, 1961, I began boot camp at the Great Lakes Naval Training Base, and upon completion, after spending Christmas leave with family and friends, I began radioman school at the naval base in Banebridge, Maryland. As with all my schooling, I struggled mightily, my dyslexia – again, self-diagnosed – constantly hindering my progress, but I persevered. In fact, during the first month of school, only one other student and I had received perfect scores on our initial exams. Five weeks later, after completing all other tests, I received a letter containing both my final scores and where I would be assigned. Breathless, convinced I had failed my final exam, I took a long time opening the letter. When I did, I saw that I had passed everything and, breathing again, that I had orders to report to the naval station on Alaska's sea frontier to serve on the admiral's staff. After nearly missing graduation ceremony that day because I had delayed so long before opening the letter, I was on my way to Kodiak Island. As the saying goes, "The best laid plans of mice and men oft go astray," and in my case, on Kodiak Island, they would go astray. Far, far astray.

Nicknamed the "Emerald Isle," Kodiak Island is located off Alaska's southern coast, 250 miles northwest of Anchorage. It is separated from the Alaskan mainland by the Shelikof Strait, named after a Russian explorer and fur trader. The largest island in the Kodiak Archipelago, Kodiak Island is the second largest island in the United States and the eighth largest in the world, with an area of slightly more than 3,595 square miles. It is ninety-nine miles long and ranges from ten to sixty miles in width. Kodiak island is also the namesake for Kodiak Seamount, which lies off the coast of the Aleutian Trench. The largest community on the island is the city of Kodiak itself.

Along with Afognak, Shuyak, and numerous other nearby islands, Kodiak Island forms an archipelago that is an extension of the Kenai Mountains. It is, therefore, mountainous and heavily forested in the north and east, but mainly treeless in the south. The island has numerous deep, ice-free bays that provide sheltered anchorages for boats. Kodiak's weather is temperate by Alaskan standards. December to March is the cold season, with average temperatures in the twenties, while June to August is the summer season, with the average high around sixty degrees. Native to the island are red foxes, black-tailed deer, elk, and over 200 species of birds, including bald eagles. Foremost, however, are the king crab and, of course, the Kodiak bear, also known as the Kodiak brown bear. It is the largest recognized subspecies of brown bear and, along with the polar bear, it is one of the two largest bears alive today. Kodiak Natural Wildlife refuge, established in 1941, covers approximately two-thirds of Kodiak Island and is the habitat of the Kodiak bear.

Commonly, the Kodiak bear reaches sizes of 660 to 1,320 pounds and has even been known to exceed weights of 1,500 pounds. Despite this large variation in size, the lifestyle and diet of the Kodiak bear does not differ greatly from that of other brown bears, such as the grizzly. An average adult male measures eight feet long and stands four to five feet at the shoulder when standing on all four legs. The largest recorded wild male weighed 1,656 pounds and had a hind foot measurement of eighteen inches. When standing fully upright on its hind legs, a large male can reach a height of ten feet.

Kodiak bears and cattle ranchers have waged a continuous battle for over 200 years. Original Russian settlers were encouraged to bring large, aggressive dogs to protect cattle from bears. As early as the 1930s, biologists and ranchers were exploring ways to reduce the number of cattle killed by bears. At one point, bears were shot from airplanes. All active efforts at bear control in Kodiak ended in the mid-1960s, around the time I was stationed on Kodiak Island.

I arrived on Kodiak Island late one night in March of 1963. The following day, I met the men I would be working with, about thirty-five in all. To this day, however, many of those men and their names escape my memory. But I liked most of them, and I liked my job because it involved anti-submarine warfare, principally against the then Soviet Union. I also liked my boss, Chief Pearson, and felt privileged – even special – to have special secret clearance on the admiral's staff.

I began my service as a seaman and after serving six months on the admiral's staff, I became a RM (Radioman) 3rd Class. The rest of the crew and I worked in twelve-hour shifts – twelve on, twelve off – for three days, followed by three days off. I spent my free time, as most of us did, playing cards, watching movies, and playing more cards, while getting to know the people around me. Once I started making friends, I played even more cards. And after that? Yup. You guessed it. More and more cards.

As a RM, 3rd Class, as I have said, I held a security clearance and worked with other radiomen who held one, also. Our job involved detecting foreign submarines in the sea frontier. To do so, aircraft would fly close to the water and lower sonar devices that would continue to be monitored from the plane. The radiomen aboard the plane would then transmit coded messages to us, which we would send, in turn, to another secure source with top-secret clearance. One of the men I worked with was Renald "Renny" Chase, a RM, 1st Class, who made Chief about the time I achieved my 3rd Class rank. Two others were Arthur Cook, another RM, 1st Class, and David Jarvits, a RM, 2nd Class. The reason I mention their names will soon become very clear to you.

Shortly after starting work on the admiral's staff, I started fishing by myself. I had bought a Mitchell 300 reel along with a spinning rod, hip boots, and fishing tackle. The salmon, true to what I had heard, were bountiful in the lakes, rivers, and streams near Kodiak Naval Air Station. The river I usually fished in was wide and so deep that, despite its crystal-clear water, I was unable to spot fish, even when one was on the end of my line near the surface. The first day out, I caught a salmon with every cast. It seemed to me as if the fish were crazed, swimming and splashing all around, their goal merely to spawn and then die. Comparatively few seemed interested in feeding. Eventually, with the fishing just too easy, I grew tired of it and sold all my gear to a friend. For the time being, my fishing career was over, but not my hunting days. Not by a long shot, if you'll pardon the pun.

While on night shift, I usually worked with David Jarvits, and sometimes with Arthur Cook. While only two of us worked at night, five or six radiomen were required during the day, among them, several officers and the admiral, himself.

RM, 1st Class, Arthur Cook, a gruff, twenty-year navy veteran, lived off base in Kodiak, where he spent much of his time reloading ammunition for all the guns he owned, among them, several high-powered rifles capable of bringing down a Kodiak bear. One day, Arthur invited me to his home to watch him reload. I was so impressed by his knowledge and skill, I wanted to learn all I could to do it myself. At the time, I did not own a gun, but Art got me started by letting me reload some of his. With thoughts of hunting a Kodiak bear growing daily, thoughts soon turning to a dream, a goal, I bought a Smith & Wesson .357 Magnum Highway Patrolman, with a four-inch barrel. Along with the gun, I purchased a hand-press with dies for the Magnum, several boxes of ammunition, gun powder, primers, and wad cullers. Having everything I needed to reload ammunition, I immediately headed to

Art's house again. Since Art and I often worked different days and shifts, soon it became too difficult to reload only there, so Art helped arrange for the boatswain's mate, who kept the barracks whistle-clean, to give me a key to his large supply closet. There, he gave me a corner where I could store everything and reload whenever time allowed.

During the daytime when I was scheduled to work nights, I usually reloaded fifty to one-hundred rounds of ammunition. I would then accompany Art to the shooting range in Kodiak. Eventually, I would go alone.

Now that I had a handgun capable of frightening a bear, I needed a rifle that would allow me to take one down. But what kind? After much thought on my part and Art's, we decided on a Savage .7mm Remington Magnum, with a belted case that packed enormous wallop in terms of pounds of energy at impact. That part of my purchase complete, I then bought a used Tru-line Jr. reloading press. Because I could only get .7mm dies that resized only for my rifle, however, I had to fire-form the shells in my gun. After I shot the ammunition I had bought, the casings would fit my rifle and I was able to resize the neck and replace the lead without having to resize the entire casing. At last, I was in business, and I could load for deer or bear as needed. For the first time ever, I aspired to tracking and shooting a Kodiak bear, the bigger the better, its flesh helping to feed the local indigenous people.

I cannot recall when I began my friendship with Renald Chase, whom we sometimes called "Renny," and sometimes "Chief," or just plain Chase. A funny, yet rather complex guy, he was a devoted family man, hunter, and fisherman. Chase and his wife Edie – an equally devoted mother – had three wonderful kids: Darrel, age eight or nine; Susie, age six or seven; and Darren, nicknamed "Cutter," about three years old. Over time, I grew close to Renny and his family, and occasionally I went camping with them for days at a time, whenever the opportunity presented itself. Chase and Edie were the first and only parents I knew that had a "No Hitting" rule. Neither parent ever spanked or struck their children in anger or frustration or to discipline them. That's how devoted both Renny and Edie were to making themselves the best parents possible and raising their children with all the respect and dignity they deserved.

One experience that I had with Chase and Edie and their kids I remember vividly. We had driven about 600 feet above sea level when we stopped and parked, prepared to climb to the top of the 3,600-foot mountain in the distance before us, where we planned to spend the weekend. With Cutter perched atop Chase's shoulders, they led us toward the mountain, Edie directly behind them, followed by Darrel, Susie, and then me.

"Come on! Keep up!" Chase would occasionally pause, turn, and shout back at us. "Don't make it such a struggle, or the bears will get you!"

As we approached the mountain top, Chase suddenly said his neck felt damp. Finally stopping, looking up at Cutter on his shoulders, he asked, although he already knew the answer, "Cutter, did you pee?" Quickly hauling Cutter down from his perch, never angry, merely annoyed, Chase walked the rest of the way with his son by his side. Soon we reached the gorgeous lake brimming with trout that awaited us atop the mountain.

Shortly after arriving at the lake, we headed to a small, slapdash shelter everyone called "Huckly's Hut," though why it was called that remains a mystery. Nobody knew who "Huckly" was. The "hut" consisted solely of a plastic tarp arranged over an alder bush to provide shelter from inclement weather and a place to keep sleeping bags and other camping gear dry. That Friday, and throughout the weekend, we feasted on trout and any other fish we caught. Life was good, but I had yet to go hunting with Chase. I wished we could. For a Kodiak bear. The sooner the better.

Climbing the mountain near the naval base was a popular activity on days off, and on another occasion, I made the trek with Chase and another serviceman whose name I fail to recall, so I'll just call him "Guy." Chase and "Guy" each carried a backpack loaded with food and equipment, and I got to go only by agreeing to carry two cases of beer in my pack. Again, at this time in my life, with thoughts of what I had told myself when I was ten – "I'll never be able to drink when I get older because I'll become an alcoholic" – occasionally echoing in my mind, drinking was still no problem for me. I was far too interested in other things, namely, learning all I could about becoming an outdoorsman. And hunting a Kodiak bear.

As the three of us headed up the mountain that day, as we neared the summit, I realized that Chase had been walking as fast as he could ahead of us – at times, practically running – until he finally had to stop, rest and catch his breath.

"You been trying to wear me out?" I asked as I finally arrived at his side, along with "Guy."

"You son of a bitch!" snapped Chase, chest pounding, face red. "I've been trying to make *you* tell *me* to slow down and take a break. And all I've done is nearly kill myself! You bastard…!"

Later that evening, after we had reached the summit and settled in, I went fishing and caught a large trout. Gloating over my catch, I showed it to Chase and "Guy" and said, "Okay, you two. When one of you gets a bigger fish, I'll take a turn fishing again. Until then, it's all up to you." I then got myself a cold beer, and for the rest of the day and the next, I watched them try unsuccessfully to catch a trout bigger than mine. All the while, I drank more beer and kept our campfire stoked. Finally, two days later, as dusk fell on a Saturday, Chase reeled in a new "King" trout, and it was my job to fish again. Minutes later, after only my second cast, I hauled in a trout bigger than Chase's and, as he threw up his hands, cussed and swore, we switched positions again and I cracked open another beer.

Things continued that way until Sunday morning when, after breakfast, "we" packed up to leave. Unlike Chase and "Guy," I did absolutely nothing, as I had nothing to pack.

"Why don't you put some of this stuff in your pack, instead of just sitting there?" Chase, visibly perturbed, groused at me.

"I don't think so." I smiled a Cheshire cat's smile. "You carry down what you carried up. That's the rule we all agreed to. I carried the beer. And since that's all gone, I don't have anything left to haul." My smile broadened even more.

We had buried all our "empties," and with nothing to encumber me, I began heading down the mountain ahead of Chase and "Guy." Soon, however, I noticed that my pack seemed heavier than it should have, and I realized that Chase must have put something in it when he helped me strap the pack on my back. When we finally arrived at our car at the base of the mountain, I removed the pack and opened it. As I did, Chase, clutching his gut, began laughing hysterically.

"What's so funny?" I barked, as Chase approached me, still laughing.

"This," he replied, and, still busting his gut, he removed two large rocks that he had placed in my pack. As he did, I realized I still had a lot to learn in life, and that I better start learning fast before I ever go out hunting for a Kodiak bear.

During the following months, along with playing a lot of cards, watching movies, and fishing, I began to spend much of my time shooting and learning to reload ammunition for my rifle. And when fall arrived, I began to hunt with a fellow card player, whose name also escaped me long ago, so I'll call him "Cards." On this outing, my goal was to get my first deer. It would not take me long.

Early one morning, "Cards" and I drove to Anton Larsen Bay in a light blue Jeep that he and two of his friends on base owned. Arriving at our destination, we left the Jeep at the end of a long dirt road. Then armed with rifles, in pursuit of deer, after scaling several high ridges approaching a mountaintop, we headed down into a large basin about a half-mile across and 300 feet below the highest ridge. Finally, we arrived in a small, wooded area, where the basin sloped down and ran towards the south. I positioned myself in the basin's southwest corner in a small grove of alders, while "Cards" trekked to the north end to take up his position.

Suddenly, as we both waited, watched for deer, I was startled by a creature's humongous black head that had appeared out of the brush about six feet ahead from where I sat. Heart hammering, I silently shouted, "A bear!" Moments later, however, I found myself staring not at a bear, but at a black Angus steer that had wandered far from its herd. Was I relieved! I smiled and watched it amble away.

Heart and mind settled, I got up and quietly made my way to the basin's eastern side. Both "Cards" and I were using the alder brush as cover to prevent deer from seeing us. I had never hunted deer before – only squirrels – so I did my best to pretend I knew what I was doing. As the Associated Press would one day say about me in its reports about my being lost on Kodiak Island, I was "definitely not a woodsman." But I could always pretend to be one.

As I positioned myself near "Cards" in a spot where we could both watch for movement on the hillside facing us, I suddenly spotted a deer about four-hundred yards away. As I lifted my rifle and was about to shoot, another deer instantly appeared near the first, and then stepped directly in front of it. Realizing that if I fired and the bullet dropped a foot over the 400-yard distance I would still hit the deer's lower neck, I took aim at the side of the second deer's head. Then gently squeezed the trigger. Down went the deer. All the time I had devoted to becoming a better shot had paid off, and as I gazed back at the first deer, it stood as still as the earth, itself. Immediately I whispered to "Cards," If you want that deer, I'll shoot him for you."

"Sure, I do!" he hissed. "But where is he? I don't see him."

Barrel blazing, immediately I took aim and fired away. Again, and again, all my shots missing their mark. The deer, unphased, stood motionless as ever, and so "Cards" was still unable to spot the target.

"I'll walk toward him," I whispered. "Watch in the general area. You'll see him move on the hillside up above me. Shoot as soon as you do. It'll be okay. I won't be in your line of fire."

Quickly, quietly, I scurried down the slope and then up the opposite slope, towards the deer. Just as I dropped to the ground, suddenly the deer moved, and "Cards" fired three shots in rapid succession. What a feeling of sheer exhilaration to hear those bullets go whizzing by, just above my head! But each shot had missed its mark. Our prey had escaped. Looking down the mountain, I saw that the deer I had shot had slid down about 100 feet from where I now stood, and that it lay dead. I would have to go get it and haul it back up the steep mountain slope.

I refused to let "Cards" help me pull the eight-point buck back up the mountain. I wanted to do it myself. Why? I didn't know back then, and I still don't. I think it was merely because it was my first deer. And I was feeling so proud of myself. I did, however, allow "Cards" to help me tie the deer to the Jeep's hood.

Ironically, as it turned out, a friend of "Cards'" who shared ownership of the Jeep had shot an eight-point buck two days earlier, and when we arrived back at the naval station the guard at the entrance said, "You clowns still driving around with that deer tied to your hood? The two of you make me sick!"

We laughed, until I explained what had happened, and that we weren't the same guys he had seen two days earlier with a deer on their hood. We all laughed hard after that.

On yet another early hunting expedition in preparation for one day tracking down a Kodiak bear, Chase and I journeyed out late one Saturday morning, again on the east side of Anton Larsen Bay. Starting late got us to the mountain top in time to set up camp and start a fire, eat supper, and sleep, which would enable us to start hunting first thing in the morning- without having to climb the mountain at daybreak. What a great plan, Chase and I both thought, except Mother Nature had other ideas. It rained all night and by morning, soaked through and through, I wanted only to return to the car and go home. Chase, however, convinced me to stay until we got a deer.

"We're already on top of the mountain, so it won't take us long to get one. Then we'll go home." Chase sought to assure me.

As things turned out, Chase was right. Both of us soaking wet, we had trudged about fifty yards when a deer appeared about that same distance away from us. We had decided I would take the first shot, and I brought down the buck with a single blast. Quickly we quartered the deer and were placing the parts in our packs when Chase said,

"That was way too quick and easy. Let's get another deer."

I refused. Cold and wet, I had had enough. Finally, Chase relented, and down the mountain we went. When we arrived back at the car, the rain had let up. We had parked at the start of Anton Larsen Bay, and as we unpacked the deer parts and loaded them into the car, Chase suddenly heard a ruckus in the alders off to our right. We decided to investigate. The trees overhung the stream that ran among the alders along the bank, so Chase, gun in hand, jumped into the water to get to where all the noise had originated. I did the same, and as I followed him, we both readied ourselves to shoot. Almost immediately, however, Chase found himself amid a swarm of walla salmon swimming upstream. The water thick with the seemingly crazed fish, Chase dipped beneath them as he made his way to the opposite bank.

"That could've been a bear we heard!" I called to Chase. "Trying to catch some salmon."

"If it was a bear, I would have scared the shit out of him coming out from under all those salmon!" he laughed.

"That's for sure," I agreed. "You would've been the biggest salmon that bear ever saw."

Chase was right, just as he was about many things. He was a smart man and was even trying to teach himself Russian. One day, I asked him why.

"So when the Russians take over the U.S.," he pretended to explain, "I will know how to say, 'Please allow me to kiss your ass.'" Of course, the real reason why Chase was learning Russian was due to his job. His clearance was top secret, and never was I allowed entrance to his area at the naval base.

Finally deciding to end our investigation into what had raised such a ruckus in the alders, we emerged from the stream and as we headed back to the car, I saw something lying in a crumpled heap on the ground to our right, about 100 yards away. As we approached it, we saw that it was a cow. Its throat had been ripped out, along with its milk bag. Close by, within two-hundred feet of one another, lay two more carcasses. Immediately Chase and I both knew a Kodiak bear had killed them, and that the bears would return in a few days to feast on what they had left, having savored the choice innards at the time of the kill.

As it turned out, the slaughtered cattle we saw were only a tiny representation of the battle bears and cattle ranchers had been waging for over 200 years on Kodiak Island. As early as the 1930s, biologists and ranchers were exploring ways to reduce the number of cattle killed by bears. At one point, bears were shot from airplanes, and a nine-foot-high bear fence was proposed to bisect Kodiak Island and create a "bear-free zone." Eventually, in the mid-1960s, all efforts at bear control ended. Maybe, I thought, I could do something about it.

The following weekend, with none of us working, Chase and I took a friend hunting with us, something we seldom did. Soon, you'll learn why. As usual, we parked at the start of Anton Larsen Bay, but on this day, we decided to head out towards Sheratin Bay to go bear hunting with "James," our friend's last name. I cannot recall his first name. Anyway, in the service, we usually called each other by our last names.

To get to Sharatin Bay involved scaling a 2,100-foot mountain – a long-extinct volcano – and then traveling down the other side towards a water-filled crater. It was far too steep to trek straight down to the water, so after reaching the summit, we decided to descend gradually by heading south, using slopes much less steep to keep our footing.

As we began our descent, however, we suddenly spotted a large herd of deer. Amid the herd was a huge buck. Instead of any bear in the area, we pondered making him our prey. And decided we would. Raising my rifle, I took aim, but Chase quickly stopped me from firing.

"Our friend James gets first shot," explained Chase, and I immediately agreed. So, James took aim as Chase and I waited…and waited… and waited for him to pull the trigger. Until it was too late. And the buck had left.

"Why didn't you shoot?" I exclaimed in disbelief. But when I turned to James, I saw that he had tears in his eyes. Though I had no empathy for him then, I do now. Disappointed, shaking my head at the lost opportunity, I silently continued the steep descent with Chase and James, until we finally reached the basin, where we spent the night. And I forgave James for what he had, and had not, done.

The following morning, we travelled to the far end of Sharatin Bay, where we spent several hours hunting bear, but to no avail, so we started back up the mountain to return to Anton Larsen Bay. For James, however, the climb rapidly turned into a nearly impossible struggle, and we constantly had to stop and wait for him to catch up.

"Either we wait, or we'll have to carry him up," Chase confided in me, both of us frustrated with our lack of progress as James fell further and further behind, his movements now like those of someone teetering on the verge of collapse.

Once we reached the summit, we waited twenty more minutes for James. Finally, he arrived - with fear on his face and more tears in his eyes - because he thought we had abandoned him. As it turned out, James would never again ask to go hunting with Chase and me. And we agreed never to take anyone with us again. Besides, after James had told everyone back at the base what had happened, and the "torture" he had experienced, no one wanted to go with us, anyway.

When we finally arrived back at the car that day, after loading our gear in the trunk, we headed back to the station. As we drove, we soon passed an old, dilapidated barn just off the road to our left. Hammered to one of its wooden-planked walls were three bear hides. Instantly Chase and I knew what had happened. The rancher whose cattle had been killed had waited for the bears to return to finish their feast. Instead, he had finished them.

In November of 1963, a severe snowstorm struck Kodiak Island. Viewed in retrospect, one event that occurred during that storm may have been an omen of what awaited me one day- if I failed to heed its warning.

A friend of Chase and mine, Lt. Robert P. "Bob" Anderson, had gone out hunting with three of his friends and had gotten lost. According to the story that circulated throughout the base, one of the hunters had shot a deer, and as he and two of his hunting companions dressed it, our friend Bob left to track two other deer that the group had spotted. About fifty yards down a slope, Bob caught up with one of the deer and shot it. By then, however, the storm had turned into a blizzard, nearly blinding all four men. Finished dressing the dead deer, one of the three men called to Bob and asked if he needed help with his deer before heading back to the truck. Bob shouted, "No!" and that they should go ahead. He would return to the truck just behind them. When the three men arrived back at their truck and waited for Bob, however, he never arrived. There was no sign of him anywhere, and no response when they called his name. Urgently, the three returned to base and announced that Bob was lost. A party of Marines stationed on the base was sent out to find him, but as day turned to night, there was still no sign of Bob.

Promptly at seven that night, a meeting was held at the Little Red Schoolhouse on the base for anyone interested in joining a search party the following day, when the weather was expected to clear. When I arrived at the old, one-room school, three men sat together at a desk to address those of us in attendance.

"So far we have three volunteers," announced one member of the trio, "but I know 'Joe Blow'" – I have forgotten his real name – "will go, even though he's not here."

Immediately I spoke up and said I wanted to go, and that "Joe Blow" should have attended the meeting if he wanted to volunteer.

"Who are you?" asked another man seated at the desk. "And where are you from?"

After introducing myself and stating that I was from the Alaskan sea frontier, the officer responded, "I meant where are you from, originally?"

"Connecticut," I answered, and the man, whose name turned out to be Ovid McKinley, granted me permission to join the morning search. Ovid also turned out to be the head of fish and game on Kodiak Island.

Early the next morning, Chase and I joined a crew on a fishing boat heading to Zerdin Point to search for Bob. Along with us were Ovid McKinley and his assistant, David Henley, and another friend of ours from the base, "Mac" McDonald. In all, there were six of us from the base, and we became known as the "Boat Six."

When we finally arrived at Zerdin Point, we went ashore by row-boat, Ovid, however, wearing high leather boots, quickly jumped into the water and walked to shore.

"Now I don't have to worry all day about getting my boots wet," he joked, easing our minds, but only momentarily.

We had come to Zerdin Point because it was close to where Bob and the other three hunters had been the day before the storm. We thought that Bob may have lost his way by trying to travel downstream to the ocean. But if the storm and the visibility had both been bad enough, he may have gotten turned around during a white-out and lost his bearings somewhere near Zerdin Point, rather than finding his way back to Anton Larsen Bay.

Later that day, during the afternoon, I discovered the entrails of the first deer one of the hunters with Bob had shot. Quickly we all cleared the surrounding area to search for tracks, but by day's end, we had found no signs of Bob. With daylight rapidly fading, a copter soon arrived to return us home.

The following morning, the "Boat Six," now known as the "Copter Six," flew back to where we had left off the previous evening to continue the search. After landing, David Henley had me partner with him, and we were all extremely careful to walk in our tracks from the day before to avoid making new ones that other searchers that had been sent out might mistake for Bob's. Quickly David and I went to the entrails that I had discovered the previous day, and after lowering himself to his knees, David placed his head to the ground, close to the innards. Then rising, he began climbing a nearby hill with about a forty-five-degree incline. As he did, the rest of us gathered and headed to where the hunters, minus Bob, had dressed out the deer one of them had killed. The area was more field-like there, with only a scattering of alders, but other searchers had obliterated what few signs we detected of what might have been a single man's tracks, namely Bob's.

As I joined him, again David kneeled, placed his head to the ground, this time telling me to do the same, which I did. Then lifting his head, he squinted at a nearby hill, examined it closely, and again told me to do the same. Following his instructions, as David continued to stare at whatever he was looking at, I finally looked up… and saw what he saw- a trail of slight indentations, footprints, heading straight uphill in the seventeen inches of snow. Were they Bob's prints? Adrenaline rushing, I scrambled to find out as David remained where he was, still on his knees, eyes peering up at me.

When I arrived near the trail of prints, David immediately instructed me to circle to my left in a half-moon shape. Then he ordered me to, "Slow down…Slow down…" followed a minute or two later by, "Now stop! Place your hand down close to the snow. Right there! Now move it a little to the right…Now to the left…Stop! Leave your hand there!" If David saw something, I had no idea what it was.

Joining me on the hill, David carefully avoided disturbing the prints. Then telling me to remove my hand from the snow, just as carefully, he brushed away the snow where my hand had been.

"See the way the grass is lying," he explained, examining the small, barren patch of turf. "It's lying in the direction your friend Bob was travelling."

We repeated the process all the way uphill, until we arrived at the top. There, almost instantly, we spotted a flock of buzzards circling above the pine tree line. When we arrived there, we discovered a dead deer, apparently the one Bob had shot, tied in a tree. Nearby were more prints. We followed them. They had to be Bob's. Only one question remained. Was he alive?

Eventually, the trail of prints took us down the mountain to Anton Larsen Bay, where we turned to our left on the bay's six-inch thick ice. The tide was out, and the ice-covered surface began to slope sharply downhill, so walking was extremely slippery and difficult, close to impossible. Apparently, it had been high tide when Bob had arrived here, so he was able to walk on the rocks, ice, and cliffs along the shore as far as he could to get back up the mountain and, hopefully, find his way back to Anton Larsen Bay.

David Henley continuing to lead the way, the tracks we followed revealed that Bob had made three unsuccessful attempts to scale the mountain once he had arrived at its base. The first set of prints we examined revealed that Bob, after failing to scale the mountain, had returned downhill carefully, in control. The second set were ragged, showing a definite lack of control, and possible frustration. The third and final set of prints nearly stole our breaths. They revealed that Bob had fallen most of the way back down the mountain.

When we arrived at where he must have stopped tumbling, joined now by Ovid McKinley, "Mac" McDonald, and Chief Pearson, we eventually picked up his tracks again on the snow-covered ice of Sharatin Bay. Because it was too difficult to walk on the ice, we had to call for the helicopter that we had travelled on to bring us "creepers" to clamp on our boots to prevent us from slipping and falling. Unable to land on the bay's surface – the ice had begun to break up in large chunks because the tide had gone out – the copter hovered just above them as Mac and Ovid went to it to get their creepers on. By the time they began to return to where the rest of us waited, a large chunk of ice had broken away, and they had to stop about six feet away, and six feet below from where we stood. Close by, Chief Pearson stood with his back to everyone while relieving himself. As he did, Mac suddenly screamed. Instantly, Chief Pearson yanking up his zipper, we all scrambled over the ice to where Mac stood frozen, mouth agape, eyes bulging.

When we arrived, we saw what had terrified Mac: three fingers, as white as the snow surrounding them, protruding up from beneath the ice. All of us stunned, breathless as we gazed down at them, we then found ourselves staring at something much worse- Bob's face, dead eyes returning our gazes about a foot beneath the ice.

A brief silence followed, and then Ovid McKinley whispered the following words in my ear, with the warning that if I ever told anyone he had, he would kill me.

"Before you go hunting with someone you cannot trust, you are better off to go alone."

By telling me that, as head of fish and game on Kodiak Island, Ovid feared he could lose his job. It was totally ill-advised to ever, *ever* go out hunting alone on Kodiak Island. One day soon, taking Ovid's secretive advice would nearly cost me much more than just my job. It would nearly cost me my life.

PART TWO
LOST AND FOUND

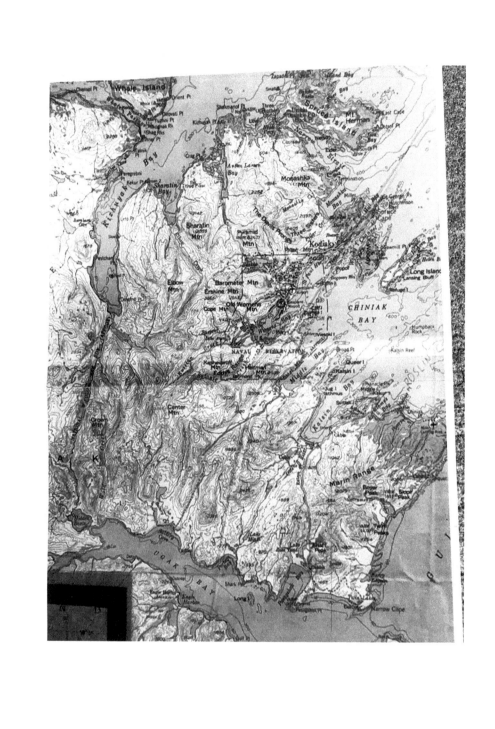

PRELUDE

"LET'S GO HUNTING!"

About ten months after Bob's body was chopped from the ice flow on Anton Larsen Bay and returned to his wife at the naval base for burial, Chase and I both eagerly agreed to go bear hunting. As there are no black bears on Kodiak Island, a fully-grown Kodiak brown bear, we further agreed, would be truly spectacular. With my three-year active duty "minority tour" nearing completion, on September 1, 1964, I was transferred from the admiral's staff to the U.S. Naval Station in Kodiak and, after a mustering-out physical, I was granted leave through September 17. Never in my wildest dreams could I ever have imagined the events that would occur during that time.

During the months that had passed since Bob's death, I had grown close not only to Chase, but his entire family. And so, now needing a place to live as a result of my transfer, after spending three days tying up loose ends, packing, and either loading or reloading my guns, on September 5, I moved in with Chase, Edie, and their three kids. Suddenly their living room couch became my bed.

On September 9, with both Chase and I in complete agreement to hunt bear and nothing else, we packed our gear and headed by car to the small airport near the naval base. From there, we hoped to hop a flight to Sharatin Bay, where we would then make our way by foot into the wilds surrounding Elbow Creek and the Buskin River, near the lake bearing the same name. We figured it would take us at least three days to ascend Sharatin Mountain near Elbow Creek and then trek down to the Buskin River before reversing our route and returning home. During that time, of course, we also planned on getting our bear. When we arrived at the airport on September 9, however, we were informed that due to the lingering fog and rain that had already gone on for several days, all flights would remain grounded. We would have to return the following day for a flight out. On September 10, 11, and 12, however, the weather remained unchanged, with all flights again cancelled. Frustrated with both the weather and our bad luck, Chase and I had no choice but to remain at the naval base and only imagine what might have been, never coming close to what reality would eventually bring- for me.

Meanwhile, Edie had left us to take the kids to Anchorage Naval Hospital, where Cutter had been scheduled for eye surgery. On the 12th, however, Edie phoned Chase to let him know that she and the kids were returning home the next day because the surgeon who was supposed to perform the operation had gone on leave without informing her or Chase that he had changed his schedule. Upon hearing the news, Chase, ever the family man, instantly grew furious and promptly informed me, "There's no way I'm going hunting with you! I'm going to stay here with Edie and the kids!"

"Come on! You can't do that!" I countered, attempting to change his mind. "We may not get another chance. My active duty tour is almost up."

But Chase had made up his mind. Not even the chance of a lifetime at getting a Kodiak bear could come close to changing it. His love and devotion to family was that unshakeable. In retrospect, I realize now how completely unreasonable, insensitive, and even selfish I had been in pleading with Chase to change his mind and come with me. Clearly, back then, especially in that moment, I believed everything was all about me. What I wanted. Nothing and no one else mattered. Therefore, in my mind, only two questions remained: Should I find someone else to accompany me, even someone I did not know and, therefore, could not fully trust? Or should I go alone?

With Ovid McKinley's words echoing in my head – "Before you go hunting with someone you cannot trust, you are better off to go alone" – it occurred to me that maybe Ovid was right. No, he *was* right. I would be better off hunting alone. After all, what could possibly go wrong? I was infallible, wasn't I? Fueled with my belief in Ovid's advice and my delusion of infallibility, I would soon discover nearly all that could possibly go wrong. And I would have no one to blame but myself.

Sunday, September 13, 1964

EARLY IN THE morning on September 13, with the fog lifting slightly and the steady rain turning to a drizzle, I walked alone to the nearby airport to check on flight departures and if any were available yet.

"Come back at noon and we'll fly you out!" an airport official informed me.

Heart leaping, hopes soaring, I practically ran all the way home to tell Chase the news. Surely, I thought, he would change his mind and come with me.

"I said I'm not going!" he adamantly reminded me, as if scolding me for thinking what I wanted could possibly outweigh his decision and crack the very foundation of his life- his family.

"Well, I am!" I instantly shot back. "Maybe someday you'll have another chance, but I might not. I'm going!"

With that, I immediately donned my coat and boots, grabbed my rifle and already loaded pack – which included extra clothing, some food, and a machete – and strapped on my pistol. And off I went. To hunt Alaska's, and one of the world's, most fearsome creatures. Alone.

Because I had no one else to trust.

After arriving at the airport, as a seaplane provided by Harvey's Flying Service prepared for take-off, I loaded my belongings into the storage compartment behind where I sat with two other passengers. With only four of us aboard, including the pilot, it took about twenty minutes for us to arrive at Sharatin Bay, where I would then head by foot toward Elbow Creek and Buskin Lake.

When we landed in the bay, the waves were large and choppy beneath the iron-gray sky, the air wet and raw. Looking out the windows, we saw that the plane's tail lay beneath a large wave, its nose directly above it. Bearing down on the throttle, the pilot, clearly experienced with such a maneuver, then levelled out the plane and motored toward the nearest bit of shore.

Upon arriving, the pilot and I got out and, together, we unloaded all my gear.

When we finished, the pilot then turned and looked me in the eye.

"Are you sure you want me to leave you all alone here?" he asked gravely.

"Yes," I instantly replied, brimming with confidence. "I am sure."

I then helped the pilot push the plane back into the water and, as it took off, I felt sure he and the remaining two passengers must have been saying, "We may not see that kid again. And maybe no one else will, either. He may be gone forever." If they were thinking and saying that, they were correct.

After watching the plane slowly disappear in the gray overcast, silence replacing its steady drone, I strapped on my backpack, slung my rifle over my shoulder and, after walking about a thousand yards, suddenly realized I was surrounded by water. The pilot had set me down on a small island. Suddenly none too pleased with him and all his "experience," I angrily paused to don my hip boots before slogging through the frigid, ever-deepening water toward the mainland. The water filling my boots as I approached the shore, drenching my feet, turning them icy-cold, though I forgive him today, I grew even more pissed-off with what the pilot had done. Then, to top things off, suddenly it began to drizzle, and with the air temperature at about forty-five degrees Fahrenheit, I felt chilled to my bones.

Later that day, when I finally arrived at one corner of Sharatin Bay, I discovered a large bear skull with the jawbone and teeth still intact. After cracking open the skull, I removed all the teeth to save as souvenirs. Today, I still have a few left. Then, after walking a mere several hundred feet further, suddenly exhausted, as darkness fell, I decided to spend the night perched in a tall pine tree. Before climbing the tree, however, I decided to first rest and eat. Removing a loaf of bread from my pack, along with a two-pound can of peanut butter and an equally sized can of strawberry jam, I made myself two sandwiches, which I quickly devoured.

Done eating, wearily, I tied my backpack to one end of a rope I had brought along, hooked and tied my rifle at the middle, and then tied the other end to my belt before climbing up into my perch, pulling my belongings up with me as I did. Once I found a "comfortable" spot, I then tied myself to the tree to keep from falling and settled in for a good night's sleep. Or so I hoped.

While all this was going on for me on the 13th, only later would I learn that as soon as Chase realized I really had gone off alone to hunt bear, he began to panic. And as the day wore on, he decided he needed to go out and find me. Save me. Because he knew I was in way over my head. And that like so many other young men my age, I was blinded by dreams and illusions and, perhaps worst of all, delusions of infallibility. In other words, I was full of myself, and that he would have to rescue me from both nature and that self. Before it was too late.

Later in the afternoon on the 13th, around the same time I was about to call it a day and climb up into my nest, Chase called Arthur Cook to tell him what I had done and what he and Arthur now needed to do – find me – before I got lost, if I hadn't done so already. Immediately Arthur agreed to take Chase to Anton Larsen Bay in the morning. From there, Chase would begin the long, arduous trek over Sharatin Mountain down to Sharatin Bay, where he hoped to soon find me. Alive and well. Unlike our friend Don.

Monday, September 14th

THROUGHOUT THE NIGHT it had rained on and off, and by daybreak on September 14, I was so drenched, cold, and miserable I decided to head home and forget about hunting bear- to hell with it all! But as I untied myself from the tree and began gathering my things to climb down, I was stunned to see two of the biggest deer I had ever seen suddenly appear about seventy-five yards away to my left. Quickly grabbing my rifle, I decided to shoot one. And then just as quickly, I changed my mind. There would have been too much damn meat to carry home with me, I realized, so I merely gazed at them as they sniffed the earth before leaving my sight.

About a half-hour after they left, feeling colder and wetter than ever, I climbed down out of the pine tree, made myself two more peanut butter and jam sandwiches, and after eating, the land as barren as the ever sunless sky, I decided again to return home. Though I would have no Kodiak bear to crow about, at least there I would be warm and dry. To lighten my load, I buried the cans of peanut butter and jam while deciding to keep the remaining seven slices of bread, a can of Spam, and a small can of B & M Baked Beans. I then began what I presumed was my way home.

As the day slowly brightened to a paler shade of gray – it was about six o'clock now – I decided to walk along the coast to get back home to the naval base. After travelling about a mile, again I spotted the huge pair of deer I had seen earlier and as I approached them, I gradually realized they weren't deer at all, but a pair of chestnut-colored horses. Only later would I learn that ranchers on Kodiak Island allowed their horses to roam free. When the ranchers wanted their horses to return to them, they would offer them grain, and then saddle them up before heading off to their destinations.

Shortly after six, I started heading upstream instead of following the coastline, using the wide-open land adjacent to the stream to follow its path. After walking for about an hour, I suddenly spotted a unique, black-collared, Kodiak brown bear about 100 yards away. Slowing, staring, as I did, the bear, about 800 pounds, spotted me. Startled, instantly it took off, ambling at first, before picking up a surprising amount of speed while heading from left to my right. Quickly I stopped, raised my .7 mm Remington magnum and squeezed off a round that knocked the bear head over heels. Breathless, heart pounding, I watched the bear regain its footing and as it did, I muttered, "Oh…shit!" Again, I squeezed off another round, and then, as if mesmerized, I watched in amazement as the bear ran, stumbled and then fell, all four of its huge paws visible as it again tumbled head over heels before scrambling to its feet and disappearing into some alders. I knew I should have kept shooting the second time the bear had fallen, and that my hesitation had cost me a chance at hitting him a third time. Breathing heavily, chest heaving, I checked my watch. It was seven o'clock. Exactly one hour had passed since I had started following the stream's path. Then gazing back at the alders, I wondered if I had killed the bear.

Hearing nothing but silence all around, about twenty minutes later, anxious and fearful, I deliberately approached where the bear had disappeared into the alders. As I did, I realized I had a decision to make. Though nearly overwhelmed with fear, should I continue pursuing the bear through the alders and hope to finish it off there if it was still alive? Or, should I walk out now and hope to eventually find a fisherman who would bring me around the island in a boat and then home, so Chase could accompany me to find the bear the following day? Surely, the bear would have died by then, if it wasn't already dead. Chase and I could then skin it and haul the carcass back with us by boat. Quickly I chose the latter. Energy renewed, breathing easily now and so firmly committed to my plan that my cold, wet clothes no longer bothered me – at least, for now – I set off to share my thrilling news with Chase. Checking my watch as I headed back toward the stream, I saw that it was now nearly eight. My journey home had begun, but as I continued, it was about to change in a way I never expected. Far from it. And I would be even farther from home.

Knowing I had to head east, I continued following the stream to its right, its waters growing steadily swifter and higher as it turned into a river and I searched for the left turn that would take me back to Elbow Creek. What I had failed to realize, however, was that Elbow Creek and the river had merged, causing the river to rush even faster now, swelling and growing deeper, it seemed, by the moment. And causing me to miss the left turn that would eventually take me home. Compounding my problems, the alders along the raging river soon grew so thick that I was forced to climb a five-hundred-foot cliff to avoid the frigid water. As I did, I quickly lost sight of the river. All the while, again failing to realize I had already missed it, that it had been flooded over, I continued hoping to find the left turn. With no sun to guide me, its face now hidden for days behind a mask of dark clouds, the river remained my sole guide for the way east.

Once atop the cliff, I spotted the river again far below me. What I had also failed to realize, however, was that when I left the river to begin my climb, it had changed direction, having taken a ninety-degree bend to my right. In other words, unbeknownst to me, I was now travelling west rather than east, the exact opposite direction from home. Rather than heading back toward civilization, I was now on my way to what had been beyond the realm of possibility to me. I was lost in Alaska, on Kodiak Island, something very few people, as I would learn later, had ever survived. And though Chase and I had used terrain maps, rather than compasses, on our hunting trips, when we had packed several days ago to go bear hunting together, Chase had put all our maps in his backpack. Only much later in the day, after having failed to find the necessary turn that would take me to Elbow Creek and beginning to sense that I was somewhat" lost, did I go to look for the maps in my pack. Removing my backpack, just as I was about to open it, my hand suddenly froze on the zipper instead. I realized I had no maps. They were all in Chase's pack. Instantly my heart sank, and my breath froze. But not for long. Even if I had missed the turn to Elbow Creek, I was confident I could still find my way back home. So, rather than panic on this, the seventh consecutive day of sunless skies and continuous rain, I sat and enjoyed lunch- a half can of Spam and two slices of bread. And though I was soaked and cold, I felt not only content but, as always, infallible.

Finished eating, I resumed walking easily again, confident all would turn out well. As I did, at some point, I don't remember exactly why or when, I casually stuck my right hand into my pants' pocket. And instantly found my fingers grasping a small, metal crucifix, and then the old set of Rosary beads that it joined. Not only had I forgotten the prayer beads were there, I couldn't even remember ever putting them there, or when or where I had first gotten them. They just always seemed to appear, and then disappear, before returning at various times in my life. I guessed this was just another of those seemingly random moments, but as I continued, convinced I would be home by tomorrow, I said the Rosary for the first time since…when? I couldn't remember that, either. Upon entering the service, I had stopped attending church, and I was never too big on God, anyway. But in the following days, while lost, I would use the beads every day to pray.

Until I finally no longer needed them. Until they no longer served a purpose. Because I had been found. As it would one day turn out, years from now, nothing could have been further from the truth.

Convinced I would again find the correct route home, and that despite missing the turn toward Elbow Creek I was still heading east, after travelling upriver and climbing to a height of about 2,000 feet, exhausted, cold, and wet, I decided to stop and spend the night on a barren piece of land. I wrapped myself up in the plastic drop cloth that I had packed, and then used my hunting knife to pin the plastic to the ground between my legs, forming a kind of tent so the rain would run off to either side of me, rather than pooling between my legs. As I struggled to sleep that night, I thought mostly of the bear I had shot. Though still excited about it and the prospect of sharing what I had done with Chase, convinced the bear had died by now, suddenly I feared another bear would find it and eat it. But as my eyes grew heavy, just before falling asleep, I decided it no longer mattered if Chase and I found it. After all, rather than return home to Connecticut when my active tour of duty was up, I could remain up here, on Kodiak Island, and get another bear. Furthermore, I would be out of the woods sometime tomorrow and on my way to tell Chase that I had gotten my first bear- or so I thought. And though I knew I had missed the turn to Elbow Creek because the river had flooded over it, I figured I merely needed to find another turn that would lead me back to the opposite side of the island and, eventually, Anton Larsen Bay Road- the road home. There was no way I could miss it. It was miles long. As I finally closed my eyes that night, my Rosary tucked safely in my pants pocket, prayers in my head, I felt at peace with myself and the world. I just didn't know I was lost. Hopelessly lost.

As it turned out, I slept fitfully that night, waking often to find myself shaking like a dog in my cold, wet clothes, repeatedly forcing myself to stop before briefly dozing off and waking again. Always shuddering. Until I finally surrendered and allowed myself to shudder. The "violent" shaking, I eventually realized that night, warmed and relaxed my entire body, and so, from that time on, I have always allowed myself to shake as much as possible when I feel cold. As I would one day discover, it is Nature's way – God's way – for warming and comforting us.

As he had promised, Arthur Cook dropped off Chase at the far end of Anton Larsen Bay Road on the 14th to begin searching for me. After crossing Sharatin Mountain down to the bay, close to where I had spent the previous evening, Chase stopped to take shelter for the night in an old, dilapidated barn that an earthquake had overturned in March of 1964. Throughout the night, Chase listened to bears busily catching salmon along the shore. Because it was so dark, however, he had no chance of shooting one. Several times he fired shots up into the starless, moonless sky, the heavens concealed behind black clouds, while calling my name. Only to hear a deafening silence in return, and the growling of the hungry, busy bears.

TUESDAY, SEPTEMBER 15TH

BELIEVING I KNEW at least approximately where I was, confident I would arrive back home no later than tomorrow, I spent much of the day trekking what I thought was south, the sun again refusing to reveal itself amid iron-gray clouds and a cold, steady drizzle. Though guideless, everything silent in the surrounding trees, hills, and mountainsides, my spirits remained high, my confidence unshaken as I eventually arrived at a stream that ran downhill through thickets of alder brush.

After following the stream for about two hours at a continuous pace, careful to always keep it to my left, eventually the alders grew too thick to penetrate, so I made my way up above the tree line and followed the stream's serpentine route from there. Once I arrived at a grassy area ahead and just below me, I headed back down toward the now swiftly running water. Estimating I was about 1,500 feet above sea level, I glimpsed the ocean far off in the distance straight ahead, the stream about a thousand feet below me as I continued on the slick, grassy slope, which grew precariously steeper the closer I got to the water. Soon, with the incline too sharp to maintain my footing, I clutched the nearly six-feet tall, hay-like grass to complete my descent. As I did, hoping every inch of the way that I wouldn't tumble and fall all the way down the wet hillside, I saw that stream had quickly turned to a roaring river. Slipping and sliding, nearly falling several times as I gripped the tall grass to anchor me, I finally decided to squat and shimmy down the remaining 300 feet to the water's edge. Once there, I decided to enter the frigid water, but as I stumbled, slid, and slogged my way through it, the water ran above my hip boots, soaking my already damp legs and feet. Deciding I had no choice but to follow the river from the opposite bank, though it was much higher and steeper than the side I was on, and I would soon have to climb it, I crossed the river and began my ascent. Getting down on all fours as I gazed up at my destination, again I grabbed at the roots of the tall grass as I pulled myself five or six-hundred feet straight uphill, my rifle slung over my right shoulder, my thirty-pound backpack feeling more like 100 pounds by now.

About two hours later, breathless and exhausted, I arrived at a spot atop the hill where I could stand and walk again. Though it remained overcast, the rain had turned to a light drizzle, and I had a clear view of the ocean and river ahead and below me. Resuming at a steady pace, it turned out to be a surprisingly easy walk back down toward both.

Along the way, stopping momentarily to survey my surroundings, I saw that I was now on a small island, about twenty feet wide and thirty or forty feet long, in the middle of the river. Several hours later, after hiking about four miles, exhausted from my now day-long journey, as the sky darkened, I decided to stop, eat, and then sleep until morning. After building a fire, I removed my drenched jeans, shirt, and boots and hung them to dry beside the crackling flames. Then I heated up my can of baked beans and ate them, along with a slice of bread. My belly warm and full, clothing dry, I dressed and saved half the beans and the remaining three slices of bread for breakfast. Figuring I would arrive home the following afternoon, the fact that I was nearly out of food failed to faze me. Besides, I thought, I could always snack on salmonberries, which I had already done several times that day- just like many other creatures, both great and small, out here on this island.

My eyelids growing impossibly heavy, as with the previous two nights, I wrapped myself in the plastic tarp, and as thoughts of home, both at the base and in Connecticut, slowly drifted in and out of mind, darkness soon replaced them and I fell fast asleep. Unaware that a different kind of darkness, one even colder, grimmer awaited me- far from the lights and warmth of my or anyone else's home, except those that lived out here in the wild. Like Kodiak bear.

Chase spent much of this day searching for me, his search, it turned out, growing more and more desperate as the day wore on. Upon leaving Sharatin Bay, following the route he believed I must have travelled, after trekking upriver for several hours, he discovered a boot print with a large number seven in the middle of it, and then several more prints, all the same. Assuming the boot prints were mine, Chase was certain that he had picked up my trail, and that he could stop searching for me because, by now, I must have found my way back home- where I lay asleep in a warm bed inside a warm house while he was out here in the cold, pouring rain, all for nothing.

Royally pissed, so to speak, growing more furious with me each step of the way, as night descended on the 15th, Chase headed back to Anton Larsen Bay Road and then home. When he finally arrived, it was midnight. He pounded on the door until Edie finally got up and opened it.

"Where is that son of a bitch?" he roared, storming inside, right past Edie, who immediately began crying.

"Bruce isn't here," she nearly screamed and cried even harder.

Stunned, heart racing, Chase stopped dead in his tracks and muttered, "Oh…shit. Where the hell is he? What am I going to do now?"

After momentarily staring at Edie, tears pouring down her cheeks, mouth agape as she clutched her face in her hands, he quickly called Arthur Cook. And hoped he would know what to do.

Wednesday, September 16th

Waking cold and hungry in the morning, I immediately ate the last of my Spam. Saving my bread, I then grabbed what remained of my beans and continued eating, until I suddenly stopped and grimaced. The can's tin lining had given the beans a distinct metallic taste. Disgusted, I set them aside and then, for some reason, looked down at my feet. And what surrounded them. Bear tracks. A bear had visited me during the night, leaving a set of prints on either side of where I had slept. Yes, I decided as I hurriedly packed, leaving the beans behind, between a possible encounter with that bear – judging by the size of the prints, they belonged to a fully grown adult – and arriving home, this was going to be one exciting day.

Soon finished packing – my pistol had worn a sore spot in my side, so I packed that, also – I slung my rifle over my shoulder and headed toward the ocean, about a mile or two away. My way home. Or so I thought.

About a half hour later, I stood at the mouth of the river on Kizhuyak Bay. And suddenly sensed, for the first time, for some reason, that I had been, and was now, travelling in the wrong direction. Looking out at the vast ocean, darker than the sky, a voice in my head – Mine? God's? – whispered that I should stop travelling to my left to get home and, instead, start travelling to my right. That *that* was the route up and over Sharatin Mountain, back down to Anton Larsen Bay Road. And home.

"You've walked the entire island and you know left is the way home," another voice – my ego – echoed in response to the first voice, and what I felt in my gut was right. In the end, my ego won out, and I continued toward the ocean, carefully sticking to my left, on my way to…? It would take me days to find out.

Eventually, I arrived at a shallow stream and entered it, again, always veering to my left while following its course. In what seemed no time at all, I was able to leave the stream and continue on dry land, positive that I would arrive home tomorrow, at the latest.

I hadn't travelled far when, upon venturing down into a gully about six-feet deep, I heard a ruckus in the trees and brush off to my left. Turning, I immediately spotted two Kodiak bear cubs. Maintaining my cool, sensing their mother was probably nearby, my initial thought was to avoid getting between her and the cubs. Quietly, I backed about fifty feet away and climbed a large, dead pine tree. As I stood watching on a limb about six feet above the ground, sure enough, the mother suddenly appeared and headed straight toward me and her cubs. Heart skipping, having no desire to harm the mother or her babies, I debated what to do. Because I had packed my pistol earlier that morning, I decided to take my rifle and fire a shot in the air to scare them away, and then remain motionless in the tree until I felt it was safe to leave. As the gunshot ripped and shattered the silence, the mother instantly roared and ran off about twenty yards before she stopped, turned, stood about eight feet tall on her hind legs, and looked back in the direction of me and the cubs. Seeing they were okay, she settled back down on all fours and bounded off, quickly accompanied by her children.

Remaining in my "observation post," a light, cold rain began to

BRUCE LACHANCE WITH MICHAEL A. MILARDO

fall as I watched the three bears pause in an area of yellow grass about five-feet high. Until the larger of the two cubs – darker brown than the smaller, which also had a band of blond fur about its neck – stopped to climb a dead pine tree, skeletal against the gray sky, about fifty yards from where I watched. Once the cub had reached a height of about twenty-five feet, looking in his mother's direction, he suddenly leaped down from the tree onto the other cub. After tumbling head over heels, the two then rose and ambled off in pursuit of mom.

Several minutes later, after watching them disappear, I climbed down from my post and headed back down into the gully where I had first spotted the cubs. As I did, I told myself, "There won't be any more bears left around here after that gunshot," and then climbed up the gully to where it ended, and I stood on level land. Where suddenly my heart stopped. About 200 feet away, off to my right, was the reason why. It was the very same reason why I was out here to begin with- a Kodiak bear. Trophy size. About thirteen-hundred pounds and ten-feet tall, if he were standing. As big as they come. Busy trying to catch salmon in a huge puddle the river's high tide had left behind.

Engrossed in his fishing endeavors, the giant brown bear failed to notice me. Suddenly breathless, heart hammering, for what seemed the first time in my life, I felt frightened as I watched the awesome beast trying clumsily to stand on a three-foot long salmon while try-ing to trap it in its massive jaws. Each time he stepped on the frantic fish, it would flip and slip away, only to be captured again in the bear's extraordinary, ham-sized claws and snapping jaws. Earlier, I had spared the mother Kodiak's life because of her cubs. But this one, I thought, was about to make my dream come true.

Ovid McKinley's main point to me when he said it was safer to hunt alone rather than with someone you cannot trust, was that if you were alone, "you would take more time to make yourself safe before firing a shot. Like climbing a tree or getting to higher ground. You would," he further explained, "think of something to get an advantage. And then do it."

Heart settling, breathing more easily, I heeded Ovid's advice and, after stealthily retreating from where I had stood, I headed for higher ground. Arriving at a spot about twenty feet above where I had stood, and approximately 120 feet away, I looked back down at the bear. Only to see that my prey had left. Heart sinking, shoulders drooping, though disappointed I smiled and thought, "What a day! Only two hours old and I've encountered four bears." And then setting off – again, unbeknownst to me, in the wrong direction – I hoped there would be more.

Following another stream to my left, though it eventually led me up a mountain, at least, I thought, it was taking me in the direction I needed to go. All day, I plodded up the roughly half-mile high mountain, often in the stream, sometimes hacking my way through thick brush. Late in the day, I spotted two more brown bears above the tree line- a large sow and a cub, about two years old, half the mother's size. Again, there was no way I was going to orphan the cub.

As evening approached on the 16th, I stopped in some alders and was about to make camp, when I heard a plane's drone overhead. As the plane appeared, it flew so low and close that I saw the pilot's face. But he did not see me. The thick alders hiding my presence, I frantically waved my arms and shouted, "Here! Here!" But to no avail. Quickly the plane disappeared, and not much longer after that, so did some of my optimism. But not my confidence. It was raining hard now, so, despite noticing that my wrists had been lacerated by all the brambles and brush I had pushed, pulled, and plowed my way through during the day, I quickly unpacked my plastic tarp. Then, using the alders to prop it up, I made a tent of sorts as shelter for the night. The "only" problem, however, was that I was on a hillside. All night long, though I was safe from the downpour, by dawn, the steady runoff had left me drenched and chilled to the bone.

As they had planned, Arthur Cook, knowing that my absence should be immediately reported to the duty officer, picked up Chase early in the morning on the 16th to drive together to the base. Once they arrived, the on-duty officer told them he could do nothing until 0800 hours on the 17th, at which time I would be officially AWOL.

Angry, frustrated, Chase and Cook spent the remainder of the 16th driving up and down Anton Larsen Bay Road, blasting the truck's horn and calling my name. In return, they heard nothing but silence. And as they spent a tense, restless night awaiting the helicopter search that would commence at 0800 hours, they began to fear the worst may have already occurred. That perhaps, unlike Don, they would never find me. Or if they did, like him, I would be dead.

Thursday, September 17th

At daybreak, I awoke cold, wet, miserable, my mood as gray and gloomy as the blanketed sky, rain dripping from the trees the only sound as I looked all about- no signs of a bear, or any other living creature, except me. Anxious, tormented by the relentless wet and cold, I just wanted to get moving and get home, the sooner the better.

Resuming the steep ascent up the mountain, I soon returned to the stream I had followed the previous day to complete the final 200 feet of my journey to the summit. Slogging through the stream, however, quickly became strenuous and frustrating as the water turned extremely milky, making it nearly impossible to see the rocks beneath my feet. Slipping, sliding, and stumbling, maybe walking a tightrope would have been easier as I often lost my balance and nearly tumbled into the water. Finally reaching the summit, high above the tree line, the terrain flattened, enabling me to leave the stream and proceed on soggy ground. Soon hungry, along the way, wherever possible, I snacked on salmonberries, grass, and weeds, the latter only after I had tasted a small sample to see if they were edible.

Plodding on, though I had ascended the mountain, I saw that I was also in a kind of valley, with even higher peaks off to my left and right. Arriving close to what I thought must be the stream's source, more like a mere hole in the ground than a small body of water or ponding site, I noticed that the water flowed in two different directions down the mountain. Travelling first upstream and then down, concluding Chase and others might be out searching for me now, I decided to stop and use a piece of cardboard from inside my pack to make a sign indicating the direction I thought I was headed due to the surrounding mountains- toward an area called Hidden Basin. Using my knife, I cut an arrow-shape in the cardboard, and then did my best to keep the sign propped up between some rocks along the stream so that if a search party did come this way, its members would easily spot the arrow to pick up my trail.

Continuing downstream, the water again turned milky, making it so difficult to maintain my footing that I left to follow the water's other route, upstream. Along the way, sometimes feeling hungry, I again snacked on nature's slim bounty – salmonberries, grass, and weeds – along with a green, broad-leafed, lettuce-like plant that I had found. After consuming three or four leaves, I stuffed the remainder in my pockets and continued walking until I suddenly spotted a willow ptarmigan, Alaska's state bird, and thought it might provide me with a nice, hot meal cooked over an open fire. The ptarmigan is an Arctic grouse that changes color from light brown in summer to snow-white in winter to camouflage itself from predators. With winter now approaching, the bird, like all grouse, chiefly a ground-dweller, stood about fifty feet away from where I had spotted it. It made no attempt to flee. Snow-white and still against a brown background, I thought the ptarmigan was an easy target. Stealthily removing my pistol, I squeezed off a shot, only to miss as the small bird instantly scurried off before taking flight close to the ground. Oh, well, I thought, as I watched it disappear, I really wasn't all that hungry, anyway. As the day wore on, however, I would be, so as I walked, I continued nibbling on the "lettuce" leaves

I had stuffed into my pockets...and in no time at all, began to feel nauseous. Nearly vomiting, stomach aching, I quickly discarded the remaining leaves, and as I journeyed the remainder of the day up the mountain, my appetite returning, while steadfastly conserving my remaining slices of bread, I resumed snacking on berries, grass, and weeds, along with a few bread crumbs from the bottom of my pack.

Late in the afternoon, as I again neared the mountain peak, it grew so foggy I could barely see my feet as I tramped along the soft, mucky ground. A short time later, overcome by an eerie feeling that I should immediately stop and avoid taking another step, that I was travelling in the wrong direction, I decided to turn and again, head back down the mountain. Toward evening, I finally stopped and made camp for the night. As darkness descended and the temperature fell, after wrapping myself in my plastic tarp, I breathed hard into it to warm myself- the same as when I was a kid, I thought, and breathed hard under the covers when my bedroom felt cold. In retrospect, I believe doing that as a kid was yet another oh-so-subtle gift from God to help prepare me for the future, specifically this moment, in this place, alone and far from home.

Soon, despite being soaked yet again, I felt warm and comfortable enough that I began to drowse off with, perhaps, two lingering thoughts in mind: Where am I, and when will I ever get home?

When I had failed to report this morning at 0745 hours, when my leave had officially expired, search operations were organized under Lieutenant Commander Robert P. Anderson, the U.S. Naval Station's assistant operations officer under Vice Admiral B.J. Semmes, Jr., Chief of Naval Personnel. Soon after my leave had expired, a helicopter piloted by Lt. Paul Wheeler flew over the area of my hunting plan – the wilderness of Sharatin Bay – as Chase and Cook had informed naval command when they reported me missing. They had also made it known that I had gone off alone, minus a compass, maps, and sleeping bag, which would later prove a source of contention, in more ways than one.

Considering that over the previous two years four hunters – all well-versed in wilderness survival and considered expert outdoorsmen – had been involved in fatal or near-fatal disasters on Kodiak Island, fears quickly grew that not only was I lost, but perhaps I was already dead. In one of those cases, two chief petty officers, both life-long hunters, set out to do some hunting in the Ugak Bay area to get their wives beaver pelts to make coats. Failing to realize the treachery of Ugak Bay, located on the northeast end of Kodiak Island, their boat floundered in seaweed before turbulent waters capsized it, and both men drowned. The second case involved our friend Bob, and in the most recent, a lost hunter, fortunate to have the required stamina to cover Kodiak's mountainous terrain, successfully returned to civilization- but barely so. All four outdoorsmen had pitted their experience against the sinister forces of nature on Kodiak Island. While one barely succeeded, the other three had all gambled and died. And with expert outdoorsmen all agreeing that chances of survival after three days lost and alone on Kodiak were either slim or none, Chase, his wife Edie, and Arthur Cook, along with the searchers aboard the helicopter, now feared that I had joined the list of fatalities. Their fears deepened toward the end of day, after Lt. Wheeler had landed the copter times to conduct brief ground searches- never finding a trace of me, or a trail that might have been mine.

Friday, September 18th

Awaking at dawn, again I found myself surrounded by a dense fog, the air chilly, moist as ever. Squinting my eyes and gazing up, however, I saw that the sky was not nearly as dark as it had been the previous days. Then as I uncovered myself from beneath the plastic tarp and stood unsteadily, I realized for the first time that I felt considerably weaker, hungrier than ever before, and I knew I was losing weight- a lot of weight, though how much I had no idea. During my mustering out physical, the corpsman attending to me had recorded my height as 5 feet, 9 ½ inches, weight 175 pounds. By my journey's end, those measurements would change- drastically. Despite feeling extremely weak and famished, however, I still felt I needed to conserve my remaining three slices of bread, and so I did.

Once I packed up and got started, I slowly hiked to where I had stopped near the mountain's summit the previous day. Peering out through the thick fog, I saw that I was near the edge of a drop-off, a water-filled crater from an old volcano far beneath where I stood, about 3,900 feet above sea level. Immediately I headed down to the water.

The descent was quick, and once I had travelled down approximately 1,700 feet, the fog began to dissipate, and I began journeying on a ridge in an easterly direction, based on where the morning sky was brightest. Still, in the chill and mist, there was no clear presence of the sun, Nature's and God's gift being that as with the previous five days, the temperature continued above freezing. There was no snow or ice, only moisture. Everywhere. Always. Both on the ground and in the sky.

With about 300 feet of visibility in all directions, estimating that I was now about 2,200 feet above sea level, I found the walking comparatively easy as I traversed a flat area of land about 200 feet wide. As I walked, however, the flatland gradually narrowed until it was barely three feet wide and extremely steep all around, forcing me to turn back and proceed to where I had initially started out. Again, following a stream, its course led me down another steep descent into a valley where, below the clouds and fog, I glimpsed the choppy, gray ocean. Feeling relieved that I could, hopes bolstered, as I headed toward the sea, I felt confident I would arrive at its edge by day's end. As it turned out, that was wishful thinking. The farther I journeyed, the rougher the terrain became, the going made even slower, more arduous and tedious by wet, slippery rock formations and steady rain. The damn, inevitable rain....

Late in the day, hungry and exhausted, the ocean still several miles off, I stopped and made camp, which meant very little. I merely stopped walking. Again resisting the temptation to devour my bread, with nothing to eat except the salmonberries and grass that remained, before sheltering myself beneath the plastic tarp, I removed my hip boots to soothe and massage my aching feet. As I did, I saw they were turning red and raw and were badly swollen. Alarmed, instantly I recalled what Uncle George had told me once concerning his experiences fighting in the Korean War- how important it was to keep your feet dry or, over the course of several days, they would begin to turn numb and, if left unattended, they would eventually rot as gangrene set in. During World War I, soldiers referred to it as "trench foot," which often resulted in amputation. Heeding Uncle George's warning, that night, and whenever I stopped to rest, I lifted my toes and heels free from my boots to both relieve the ache and keep them as dry as possible. Thank God for Uncle George, the man who had taught and cared about me so much.

At 5:30 a.m., two ground search parties, led by Marine Captain Gordon R. Johnston, Marine Barracks executive officer, and Ovid McKinley, head of the Kodiak division of the Alaska Department of Fish and Game, were flown out from the naval base to begin an intensive combing of the Sharatin Bay-Elbow Creek terrain. Overhead, Lt. Wheeler's helicopter flew serial reconnaissance.

Throughout the search operation – and the ones that would ensue over the following days – helicopter flights were severely hampered by the low-hanging clouds and rain. On this day, however, the 18th, Lt. Wheeler's helicopter contacted Lt. James Kaiser, who, along with his father, had set up camp on September 15 at the mouth of Elbow Creek. They reported having seen signs of a hunter pursuing a bear in the area of Kizhuyak Bay, far from Elbow Creek. Armed with this information, a helicopter search party was quickly dispatched to the area. Soon, footprints were discovered, which Chase, who was aboard the copter, identified as mine. He happened to spot the number "7" in the prints when his buntline magnum accidentally fell from his holster into one of them as he was returning to the copter. In hindsight, I now view this "accident" and Chase's gun landing in my footprint as nothing less than what I call a "God moment." A moment of divine intervention, far more than mere coincidence or accident, that would eventually result in my life being saved. Knowing they had picked up my trail, members of the search party followed the prints. Eventually, they led to an area which included sheer drop-offs and dense, jumbled scrub growth, where, much to the searchers' dismay, they immediately lost my trail, along with much of their hope.

Saturday, September 19ᵗʰ

Physically drained from my previous day's travel and the toll it had taken on my cold, aching feet and legs, I awoke at dawn having slept well. Immediately I went to the stream and stood in the water, boots still on, to soothe the pain in my swollen ankles, toes, and heels. Fearing that if I removed my boots I wouldn't be able to slide them back on due to the swelling, I decided to leave them on. Minutes later, feeling relieved, more relaxed, I returned to my "campsite." Then, after packing up my plastic tarp, I set off in the stream toward the ocean and, I hoped, home, the Rosary in my pocket a continual source of hope.

Travelling in the stream, I tried my best to negotiate its rocky bottom without renewing the inflammation in my feet and blistered legs. Again, abstaining from my bread, with salmonberries, grass, and weeds as my nourishment, at least I always had an abundance of fresh water to keep me hydrated. As with the previous day, I knew for certain from my ever-increasing weakness and fatigue that I was losing weight, each step I took more painful, ponderous than the previous. Despite my tribulations, however, my belief that I would survive never wavered, my

Rosary and prayers always there to buoy my faith and self-confidence.

After trudging along in the stream for about an hour, I finally arrived at an area devoid of large, slippery or small, sharp-edged rocks, the water's soft, muddy bottom a soothing cushion for my feet, enabling me to travel at a much easier, steady pace. Toward the middle of the day, as I neared the ocean, I was surprised by two deer, a mother and baby, that suddenly appeared, as if out of nowhere, from behind me. Unafraid, they continued walking at the same pace I did, the mother about twenty feet away on the bank to my right, the doe, minus her spots, half the mother's size, a mere four feet away from me. And then, as we continued our walk, the doe came even closer, just a foot away as it extended its neck and smelled my outstretched hand.

"What a pretty baby," I said softly, even managing a smile as my heart drummed faster with the beauty and thrill of the experience. Though, of course, I had talked silently to both myself and God over the course of the previous days, I had never spoken aloud, and the sound of my voice suddenly startled both me and the doe. Instantly she moved away to the water's edge, close to her mother, both now about ten feet away. Together, they accompanied me from that distance all the way to the ocean's shore. Once we arrived, as I continued to my left near the water's edge, they finally journeyed off to my right. I never saw them again, though to this day, in fond and meaningful memory, I always have and will. May God bless them both.

With my journey far easier now that I was walking on sand, the shore stretching out about three miles ahead of me, I maintained a steady pace in what I hoped was the right direction home. That is, until I finally arrived at a high cliff that extended out into the ocean, forcing me to leave the beach and return to higher ground. As the day wore on, again following a stream, I hoped for a quick return to the sandy shore, but to my dismay, I experienced no such luck. Eventually, as evening neared, completely exhausted, I stopped and made camp for the night. Sitting at the stream's edge with my boots on, nibbling a few berries and grass, I dangled my again swollen, aching feet in the swiftly running water in a desperate attempt to soothe them. Finally feeling better, shrouded in silence – the babble of the rushing water muffled by the wet ground and thick brush – I decided to lie down. And then, minutes later, darkness descending, I suddenly heard music and people, clearly a man and a woman, talking. Momentarily breathless, heart beating faster, I wondered if they were real, or if I was hallucinating. Losing my mind.

"Oh, you don't have to worry now," said the female voice. "Nobody will hear us way up here." But where were the two, I wondered, if they were anywhere at all, except in my head. Was the woman talking to me, or the man she was with? Were they real? My heart drummed even faster, and suddenly I shouted, "Hey! Can you hear me?" and waited for a response. Nothing. No voices. Only music.

Grabbing hold of my pistol, I fired three shots straight up into the night sky. Instantly the music stopped. Then, moments later, I heard the woman's voice again, asking the same question I had been asking myself for days.

"What are you going to do now?"

"Can you hear me?" I yelled in reply. And then waited again. Nothing but a return to silence. Deafening silence. Spirits and shoulders drooping, heart and breath easing, several minutes passed as I contemplated what had just happened. Deciding to lie down, I tented myself in my plastic wrap. Then, as my eyelids grew impossibly heavy and I drifted off to sleep, I tried to convince myself that I wasn't going insane, that the voices were real. Weren't they…?

The desperate search for me resumed at 6:30 in the morning, with the addition of two more parties led by Chase and YNC R.J. Rathbone. Tracks found late in the day led both parties to the Kizhuyak Bay area. A light helicopter-ground search was also conducted in the Ugak Bay-Hidden Basin area with the possibility that I had traversed the island there. As evening fell, hoping to spot a campfire that may be mine, a night air helicopter search was also conducted, all to no avail. Moreover, flooding marsh waters and heavy rains had completely covered the trail searchers had discovered the previous day.

With nothing but negative results, just before midnight, at 11;55 to be precise, Vice Admiral Semmes, Chief of Naval Personnel, sent a telegram to my parents in Avon, Connecticut, regretfully informing them that I was missing...

"...as a result of failing to return from a hunting trip while on leave. He was last seen 13 September when beginning his trip alone... You may be assured that every effort is being made with personnel and facilities available to locate your son...I join you in fervent hope for his eventual recovery alive..."

Due to the time difference, my parents received Vice Admiral Semmes' telegram early the following morning, Sunday, and, along with it, the complete and utter shock it would bring. The terror that they would never see me again. That I was lost to them forever. That I was dead.

CLASS OF SERVICE
This is a fast message
unless its deferred char-
acter is indicated by the
proper symbol.

WESTERN UNION
TELEGRAM
W. P. MARSHALL, PRESIDENT

SYMBOLS
DL = Day Letter
NL = Night Letter
LT = International Letter Telegram

SF-1201 (4-60)

The filing time shown in the date line on domestic telegrams is LOCAL TIME at point of origin. Time of receipt is LOCAL TIME at point of destination

1155P EDT SEP 19 64 BA007

RA001 WC253 WNRA002 XV GOVT PD WUX NR WASHDC 19 SEPT 915P EDT

JOSEPH AMBROSE LACHANCE   REPORT DELIVERY

46 SECRET LAKE ROAD

AVON, CONN

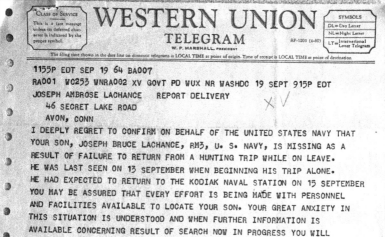

I DEEPLY REGRET TO CONFIRM ON BEHALF OF THE UNITED STATES NAVY THAT
YOUR SON, JOSEPH BRUCE LACHANCE, RM3, U. S. NAVY, IS MISSING AS A
RESULT OF FAILURE TO RETURN FROM A HUNTING TRIP WHILE ON LEAVE.
HE WAS LAST SEEN ON 13 SEPTEMBER WHEN BEGINNING HIS TRIP ALONE.
HE HAD EXPECTED TO RETURN TO THE KODIAK NAVAL STATION ON 15 SEPTEMBER
YOU MAY BE ASSURED THAT EVERY EFFORT IS BEING MADE WITH PERSONNEL
AND FACILITIES AVAILABLE TO LOCATE YOUR SON. YOUR GREAT ANXIETY IN
THIS SITUATION IS UNDERSTOOD AND WHEN FURTHER INFORMATION IS
AVAILABLE CONCERNING RESULT OF SEARCH NOW IN PROGRESS YOU WILL
BE PROMPTLY NOTIFIED. I JOIN YOU IN FERVENT HOPE FOR HIS EVENTUAL
RECOVERY ALIVE. I WISH TO ASSURE YOU OF EVERY POSSIBLE ASSISTANCE

TOGETHER WITH THE HEARTFELT SYMPATHY OF MYSELF AND YOUR SONS
SHIPMATES AT THIS TIME OF HEARTACHE AND UNCERTAINTY. IF I CAN
ASSIST YOU PLEASE WRITE OR TELEGRAPH THE CHIEF OF NAVAL
PERSONNEL, DEPARTMENT OF THE NAVY, WASHINGTON, D. C. 20370.
MY PERSONAL REPRESENTATIVE CAN BE REACHED BY TELEPHONE AT
OXFORD 42746 DURING WORKING HOURS AND OXFORD 42291 AFTER
WORKING HOURS.
VICE ADMIRAL B J SEMMES, JR CHIEF OF NAVAL PERSONNEL

CFN RM3 13 15 20370 42746 42291

,

hat followed,
s trail and
ys afterward,
horseshoe pat-
ering into the
rancher Ron

with the ele-
edly lessened
perature never
ng during his
as the rain. A
rain that is
lbe. It never
n the wet sea-

ed something
'I was lost."
days, he ate

Sunday, September 20th

AFTER YET ANOTHER night of sound sleep induced by hunger and exhaustion, I awoke for the first time with what was, for me, a feeling I had rarely, if ever, experienced before: a growing sense of dread, of complete and utter depression. Sluggishly, weak all over, far more exhausted now than hungry, I uncovered myself from beneath the plastic tarp and forced myself to eat. Reaching into my pack, I removed my three slices of bread. The mushy bread crumbling in my hands as I chewed, again I pondered the voices I had heard the previous night. Convinced they were real, that I hadn't been hallucinating, I concluded the voices were those of a man and woman in a four-wheel drive vehicle, out having an affair, and that they must have feared I was the woman's husband or boyfriend. After all, "What are you going to do now?" the woman had said, after I had fired three shots. The total silence that ensued must have meant they drove off, afraid that I would next shoot them. It all made sense, I thought and, no, I hadn't been hallucinating. But as I finished eating and then packed up, my heart sank, and my depression returned. I had contacted civilization. I had come close to rescue, only to be cheated, by two cheating lovers. Salvation, and home, were still a long way off.

Praying, Rosary in hand as I battled my depression, I headed down to the ocean to continue hiking on the soft sand. Soon running out of beach to walk on, however, as the path turned to rock and brush, I returned uphill to the stream, only to find the terrain there more rugged than ever. Nowhere else to turn, legs heavy, mind weary, I decided to leave the stream and fight my way through what seemed a never-ending tangle of alders, my thoughts, again inundated with fear and hopelessness, just as tangled. Where was all my confidence? What had become of my infallibility? All that I had ever believed about myself was crumbling before me, like the final slices of bread I had eaten that morning, with each painful, hesitant step I took- toward where?

Resting frequently, breathless, wet, weak and cold, as the day wore on, the blisters on my legs and feet worsened- excruciatingly so. Life had become nothing but a tangle of alders. Grasping their limbs for support, more exhausted, more drained of both hope and energy than ever with each passing moment, each passing hour, I experienced what I gradually realized *were* hallucinations. I began seeing old friends before me, as if they were on television. Observing these friends on the "screen," I conversed with them, sometimes silently, sometimes aloud. At one point, I saw one of them, I'm still not sure who it was, go to a shiny, white refrigerator. Immediately I asked for a glass of milk. Then, as it was handed to me, as I reached out to take it, the hand clutching the tall glass of milk instantly vanished. And I stood still, wondering if the last of my sanity had left with it. No, I decided, it hadn't, and thinking of my Rosary, praying once more, I knew I must go on.

Toward the end of the day, after hours of getting what seemed like nowhere, as night fell, I wished only to sleep. To escape not only my depression, but everything. Including this miserable place. Where even an atheist would learn to pray.

Shortly after daybreak, Captain Gordon Johnston and the rest of his search party boarded their helicopter to comb the beaches along Kizhuyak Bay, hoping to pick up my trail. Simultaneously, ground search parties scoured the terrain inland from the bay, once again, all to no avail.

Back home in Avon, Connecticut, around the same time the search parties were out looking for me, my mother and father arrived home from church. Immediately they spotted an U.S. Navy car parked in front of the house. Sensing something "bad" may have happened to me, each stood breathless as the navy representative got out of his car and approached them, Vice Admiral Semmes' "we regret to inform you" telegram in his hand. After exchanging introductions, as my parents, still breathless, read the wire, their hearts also seemed to stop. Shaken to their core, they went inside and quickly began calling everyone in the family to tell them what had happened- that I was lost, thousands of miles away, somewhere in the wilderness on Kodiak Island. Filled with their own panic and fear, everyone soon gathered at the house, their excited chatter focused solely on me- along with giant bears, bloodthirsty wolves, and any other life-threatening danger they could possibly think of. Much of the talk about wolves was initiated by my father's brother, my Uncle Paul, all of it only adding to my parents' horrible fear. Both seeing and feeling their distress, my uncles George and Freddy urged them not to worry, that somehow, I would be okay, and that together, they would fly to Kodiak as soon as possible to help find me. Though they, along with my sister and the rest of the family tried their hardest to comfort my parents, what my Uncle Richard – one of my mother's brothers – did absolutely infuriated her. He came up with the bright idea of calling a local radio station – WPOP, 1410, on the dial – which was offering $14.10 for the week's best news story. After checking with the U.S. Navy to verify what Uncle Richard had reported, having initially referred to me as "Bruce Lachance," with a lower-case "c," the navy informed the station that it had no one from Connecticut by that name. By week's end, the spelling correction having finally been made, the station announced that it was the week's "winning" story, and that "POP" would continue making hourly calls to the naval base on Kodiak to get updates on the search, all of which only fueled my parents increasing fear and anguish toward Uncle Richard.

Later in the day on the 20th, Vice Admiral Semmes sent another Western Union telegram to my parents, this one informing them that a previous ground search party had found a trail that I had apparently made on September 15 at Kizhuyak Bay. The telegram further stated that "...this last sign indicates Bruce was walking with even strides," and that day and night searches would continue. At least, for now, amid their hurricane of emotions, my parents had a flicker of hope that I was at least still alive.

908A EDT SEP 20 64 BA048 PA030

RA038 WD017 W NRA002 XV GOVT PD WUX NR WASHDC 20 SEP 836A EDT

MR JOSEPH AMBROSE LACHANCE

46 SECRET LAKE ROAD

AVON CONN

THE LATEST INFORMATION RECEIVED CONCERNING YOUR SON INDICATES
THAT A GROUND SEARCH PARTY LOCATED HIS TRAIL WHICH APPEARS TO HAVE
BEEN MADE 15 SEPT AT KIZHUYAK BAY, KODIAK ISLAND. THE LAST SIGN
INDICATES JOSEPH WAS WALKING WITH EVEN STRIDES. AN AIR AND
GROUND SEARCH IS CONTINUING DURING DAYLIGHT HOURS AND A
NIGHT AIR SEARCH WAS PLANNED 19 SEPT FOR POSSIBLE CAMPFIRE.
YOUR SON HAD A FIVE DAY SUPPLY OF FOOD AND THERE WERE
BERRIES AND FISH READILY AVAILABLE IN THE AREA.
FURTHER ICFORMATION WILL BE REPORTED TO YOU UPON MY RECEIPT.
    VICE ADMIRAL B J SEMMES, CHIEF OF NAVAL PERSONNEL

TELETEX

THIS MESSAGE RECEIVED DIRECT
FROM SENDER VIA W.U. TELEX

1964 SEP 22 PM 8 11

R 221315Z

60 TLX

FM BUPERS

TO RUETDH/MR AND MRS JOSEPH AMBROSE LACHANCE

46 SECRET LAKE RD

AVON COZF CONN

INFO RUECUC/COMTHREE

RUETDH/NAVMARCORESTRACEN HARTFORD CONN

BT

UNCLAS

A REPORT JUST RECEIVED STATES THAT A TRAIL ABOUT THREE DAYS OLD WAS
LOCATED ON 21 SEPTEMBER 1964. YOUR SON HAD LEFT A SMALL PIECE OF
CARDBOARD WITH AN ARROW CUT INTO IT INDICATING HE WAS HEADING TOWARD
HIDDEN BASIN. THE GROUND PARTY HAS REACHED HIDDEN BASIN AND REMAINED
THERE OVERNIGHT. THE SEARCH BY AIRCRAFT AND THE GROUND PARTY WILL
RESUME AT NEXT LIGHT IN THE UGAK BAY AND KILIUDA BAY AREA OF KODIAK
ISLAND. YOU ARE AGAIN ASSURED THAT EVERY EFFORT IS BEING MADE TO
LOCATE YOUR SON AND THAT YOU WILL BE INFORMED WHEN FURTHER INFORMATION
IS AVAILABLE.

VICE ADMIRAL B J SEMMES, JR., CHIEF OF NAVAL PERSONNEL

BT

Monday, September 21ST

As ALWAYS, IN the endless stream of wet, cold, gray mornings, I awoke at dawn, drained of drive and motivation, hoping, praying the sun would finally show itself. What a glorious miracle that would be! One that would certainly help to soothe not only my tormented spirits, but my blistered legs, sore, swollen feet, and wrists now raw and scabbed where thick bush and alders had lacerated them. Emerging from beneath my plastic, belly shrunken, groaning, ribs starting to protrude, I knew now that I had lost considerable weight, along with much of my hope. Yet, not my confidence. Sticking to my belief that everything would turn out all right, I maintained faith in both myself and God, especially when I said the Rosary. I had never liked asking for anyone's help, including His. For me, asking for help was a sign of weakness. Of personal failure. Of surrender. Someday, many years from this one, oh how that would all change. And what a glorious miracle that would be! But for now, it was just me and Him and the vast silence all around.

After having decided to go back to sleep, I awoke again sometime later to the warmth of a hazy sun peeking out from behind a thin curtain of clouds and fog directly overhead.

"Bruce, you have to get up now," I told myself. "You have to get going, or you're going to die."

With that warning, mustering what remained of my waning strength and energy, and, above all, my will to survive, I unwrapped myself from beneath the plastic. And then, bolstered by the sun's appearance, as if absorbing its energy both physically and spiritually, I jumped up, packed, and set out, hoping and praying that I was heading home. Proceeding downhill, eventually I made my way out of the thick alders to a large area of marshy land. Though unable to see the ocean, at least I knew I was at or near sea-level. And that this was a day separate from all the others- because of the sun. And I was alive to appreciate it.

With the wetlands stretching out before me, as I slogged along through them, soon I was forced to use the myriad of beaver dams as bridges to bits of dry land, where the going was much easier. As the day wore on, however, more and more it seemed as if I were making my way through a maze. No sooner would I begin plodding along atop one dam, when it would suddenly end, forcing me to turn back and find another one that would hopefully take me to dry land. Though wet and chilled, at least I wasn't freezing, I thought. Plus, I had the sun's rays to warm me, even though its usefulness as a directional tool was now slightly limited. I knew the sun rose over the naval base and the town of Kodiak, and thus I was heading east. But by now, all I wanted some good, hot food, an end to this madness, and someone to take me home. Salmonberries, grass, and weeds remained my only sustenance, along with fresh water.

After a maddening day of travel through the seemingly endless maze, again drained of energy, frustrated and weaker than ever – if that were now possible – I finally arrived at a stream and a stretch of dry land that ran alongside it. Feeling I could barely stand, that my knees would buckle at any moment and I would fall, I decided to stop and spend the night. Lowering myself beside the stream, breathing slowly, heavily, I allowed the cool water to soothe my throbbing feet, and at least that felt good.

How much time had passed, I have no idea, but suddenly I heard what reminded me of the humming, grinding sound made by generators to start airplane engines. And voices. Two men talking. Heart and mind exploding, suddenly bursting with hope and energy, quickly I grabbed my pistol and fired three shots in the air. And then shouted as loud as I could- "Hey! Hey!" And then waited. Nothing. No response. I wondered what was going on and thought that, perhaps, I had arrived at a top-secret military installation at the end of an island no one was supposed to know existed. Immediately I fired three more shots, yelled again.

"Hey! Hey!" Nothing but silence. No voices. Even the sound of generators had disappeared. Hopes crushed, again I wondered if I was hallucinating, losing my mind. And when and how this would all finally end. The nightmare seemed endless. As darkness descended, sleep and prayer remained my only solace. My only answers. And after wrapping myself in plastic, clutching my Rosary, sleep's black curtain abruptly fell, ending day nine, lost and alone, starving on Kodiak Island.

During the day, the hopes of ground searchers were suddenly bolstered when they discovered the cardboard sign I had made with an arrow cut into it indicating the direction I intended to travel- inland from Kizhuyak Bay. In another Western Union telegram, Vice Admiral Semmes quickly informed my parents what had happened, and that the arrow pointed away from the bay, across Crown Mountain, toward the Hidden Basin area, where Chase and other searchers, both ground and air, now suspected I was heading.

With the distinct probability that I was now somewhere in the Ugak Bay-Hidden Basin vicinity, LCdr. Robert P. Anderson ordered all units to the area. As air and ground parties converged further inland, a tugboat steamed around Kodiak, heading toward Kiliuda Bay, just below Ugak Bay, in case I had journeyed to my right upon reaching Hidden Basin. The tug was due to arrive the next morning, on Tuesday.

Also in his telegram sent this day to the U.S. Navy and Marine Corps Training Center in Hartford, Connecticut for delivery to my parents, Vice Admiral Semmes again assured them that "…maximum effort was being exerted to find me, considering rugged terrain, weather, and personnel safety." As with my parents, sister, and all other family members, Chase and everyone else in the search parties just hoped they would find me alive.

Tuesday, September 22ND

WAKING LATER THAN usual, though weak, hungry, my swollen feet more painful than ever, my will to survive pressed to its limits, I just wanted to get moving. Peering out at the gray-blanketed sky from beneath my tarp, I saw the morning had begun much the same as the previous eight. It was how the day would end that would make it different from all the others.

Emerging from beneath my "tent" in a light mist, immediately I hobbled over to the stream to soak my raw, blistered feet and ease the soreness from my legs, also blistered where tangles of brush had tattered my jeans over the course of the previous days. As I loosened my toes and heels in my boots and sat gazing up at the heavens, I saw the gray shroud overhead promised nothing new, no sun to lift my spirits, no warmth to ease the constant chill, no sign of hope anywhere that might signal an end to my journey, now entering its tenth day. Then turning away, I scanned the wilderness around me, funereally silent, nearly as barren as the ocean off in the distance, its iron-gray sheet matching the sky. As the stream's icy-cold water eased my physical pain, I wondered how much longer I could continue.

"You must," answered my inner voice, and as I eased my feet back down into my boots, at least I had my prayers and Rosary to bolster my confidence and will to survive. Somehow, some way, my journey would end, and everything would be all right. And though I still clung to my belief that I was infallible, I also realized that I needed God's help to save me, and I prayed He would.

Wearily, my feet and legs heavier than ever, seemingly more ponderous with each step I took, I headed downstream atop a precarious path of slippery boulders and sharp, jagged rocks, until I finally arrived soaked and cold at the ocean's edge. Its soft, sandy shore a welcome relief, turning left, I saw nothing but barren beach stretched out before me, no mountains to scale, no alders to tear my way through, no further punishments – other than the ones I had already suffered – for daring to challenge nature and Kodiak Island. Alone. Nothing but clear sailing as far as the eye could see, all the way home. Or so I continued to hope and pray.

Wincing from the stinging jolts in my feet and legs – I could only wonder how raw and badly blistered they were – breathing deeply the damp, chilly air, striving to renew my strength with its freshness, I set out along the ocean's edge. Constantly, I gazed off at the trees in the distance to my left searching for signs of human life, all the while fingering the Rosary in my pocket and praying to God. Until, after having travelled approximately two miles from where I had started this morning, I spotted what I hoped was not an illusion. A plume of smoke rising above the treetops, less than a mile away. Momentarily stunned, I stopped and stared at it. And then headed straight toward it. It was no illusion.

Mesmerized by the steady, rising stream of smoke, about a half-hour later, I saw what looked like a barn that had been tossed upside-down suddenly appear in the distance before me. A remnant from the earthquake this past March, I concluded, just like the barn where Chase had spent the night after travelling fourteen hours in search of me.

Breathing heavily, plodding on as my heart began to beat faster with hope, I told myself, almost jokingly, "That's no bear waiting to eat me for breakfast." I nearly chuckled, but I hurt too much to even do that. I just hoped my legs wouldn't give out before arriving at the source and reason for the smoke somewhere beyond the barn. Maybe it was God or Heaven-sent, I thought. I only knew it was real.

Nearing the overturned barn, about a half mile from the smoke, suddenly I noticed an empty beer can on the ground nearby. And then perceived what appeared to be about a thousand more piled high off to my left. No, make that about ten thousand more as I drew closer, until I realized I was staring at a very large sand dune completely littered with them. Scaling the dune, sometimes on all fours, upon reaching its summit, suddenly I spotted the road I had been searching days for, and my heart leaped. At long last, I was on my way home!

Scrambling down the sand dune toward the road, bursting with renewed strength and hope, after walking a few hundred yards, suddenly I realized I was travelling away from the smoke. Taking a quick right turn off the road, I hiked through thick woods until I arrived at a barbed wire fence. Quickly I removed my pack and hung it on the fence, along with my rifle, so I could climb over it without getting tangled. After escaping the barbs and resuming my hike through dense alders and thickets of brush, finally I arrived at a stream with another stretch of barbed wire running across it. This time, however, I merely ducked under the wire before plowing ahead, only to encounter a third stretch of wire shortly later. There was no way this one would stop me. Beyond it stood a cabin, built on stilts about three or four feet high, to avoid abnormally high ocean tides and resulting floods, I presumed. Quickly I made my way over the fence, careful to avoid getting tangled, and headed straight for the cabin door. Once there, exhausted, immediately I removed my pack and rifle, leaned them against a post. Knocked on the door. And anxiously awaited a response…

Moments later, I heard footsteps. And then a man opened the door. "I have a problem," I muttered, chest heaving as I gazed into his eyes.

No sooner had the words left my mouth when the man replied, "Is your name LaChance?"

"Yes," I blurted, astonished that he knew my name.

"You have a lot of people out looking for you," he explained. "My name's Ron Hurst. Come on in and get out of those wet clothes."

My ten-day journey lost and alone on Kodiak Island instantly over – miraculously so in my eyes and, in the coming days, the eyes of most others – I stepped inside the entranceway. Then after he closed the door behind us, I followed Ron up five wooden steps into the warmth and comfort of his home. In hindsight, perhaps those five steps marked the beginning of my next journey in life, one that would continue many years from now and, in the long run, would involve its own life and death struggles against an enemy vastly different from nature, but one every bit as deadly. And far more devious. But at that moment, basking in the warmth and simple pleasures of Ron's home, I was just glad to be alive. I still am.

Standing inside the 24' x 24' cabin, a waft of warm air from a giant, two-oven, cast-iron stove, like a warm summer breeze, bathing every exposed part of me, I breathed easily, appreciating not only the warmth of the fire but the smell of burning wood. The simplest of pleasures. The simplest of miracles. As were all the other comforts we so easily take for granted. Before me and off to my right was the plainest of kitchen tables – how long had it been since I had sat at a table with Chase and his family, enjoying their companionship – set before a large picture window that looked out to the ocean whose shore I had wandered just hours ago, as well as the woods and barbed wire fencing that now represented the final hurdles I had to overcome before returning to civilization. Alongside the table and its four chairs – what a wonderful feeling to sit on something dry and comfortable – was a protruding wall and bookshelf. Atop the shelf sat a ham radio, and behind it, on the opposite side of the wall, was Ron's bedroom. Oh, my God, to lie in a soft, warm bed again! What a feeling that would be! And what a joy!

As I stood marveling at all these simple pleasures, soaked head-to-toe, Ron opened the door to an anteroom chock-full of logs he had cut and stacked for the coming winter. Atop the wood was a clean pair of long johns that he had hung to dry.

"Get out of your wet clothes," said Ron, taking down the long johns, handing them to me. "You can wear these."

Enormously appreciative, I said, "Thank you," and began to remove my drenched, tattered clothes. First to go were my hip boots. I had not removed them since the night of the 15th and the morning of the 16th. Once off, I saw the extent of my blisters- they covered my feet and legs from toes to just above my knees, everywhere the hip boots were supposed to have protected them. Then removing my jeans, wherever brush and thorns had ripped them, my legs now bore scratches and cuts, some of them scabbed, others still raw.

After donning the fresh, warm long johns – Oh, what a pleasure that was! – I sat in a chair looking out the picture window, my back to the stove as its blast of heat threatened to turn my legs to a pair of crispy critters. But why should I care? I only knew how good the heat felt, how good everything felt.

Several minutes later, however, as I attempted to straighten and stretch my legs, I realized I could not. Along with the cuts and blisters, days of walking, crouching, and sitting, constantly drenched and cold, had now left my legs stiff, cramped, and weak. Ron and I both hoped the heat would soon ease my temporary "paralysis" so that I could enjoy the pleasure of bending and stretching again.

As I sat breathing easily, enjoying the warmth, Ron suddenly said, "I'll be right back," and out the door he went. I watched him head down to the ocean and then, about ten minutes later, I watched him return. Immediately he explained why he had left. He had placed one of three 12' x 3' pennants – a red one, the other two being blue or yellow – atop the roof of a small barn alongside the cabin. The red pennant acted as an emergency signal for any aircraft flying overhead, indicating help was urgently needed. I no longer recall what the blue and yellow pennants signified. Perhaps, if I do remember correctly, the blue one meant that Ron needed a lift into town; the yellow meant only to stop, if possible. Again, I am unable to clearly recall their significance.

No sooner had Ron finished explaining what he had done, when a small, low-flying navy plane buzzed by above the cabin before heading out toward the ocean. Immediately Ron ran out the door again and, like the plane, headed down toward the ocean. Minutes later, he returned carrying a note attached to a wrench that the pilot had dropped from the plane. The note instructed him that if "LaChance is there, lay your pennant on the ground," which Ron explained to me he had done while outside.

Seconds later, the navy plane again buzzed overhead. And again, Ron was out the door and down to the beach, before returning with a second note the pilot had dropped. This one read, "If LaChance needs medical attention, lay your pennant on the ground." What Ron had not explained to me and now did, was that he also had a small red flag which he called a pennant, and it was that he had lain on the ground in response to the pilot's second note. Then, after the plane buzzed overhead and out to sea a third time, a final note was dropped informing us that there were no medical personnel aboard, but that another plane would soon arrive with a medical corpsman as part of its crew.

Just as the note had promised, five minutes later, we saw a Coast Guard seaplane land in the ocean. As I sat and watched, Ron hurried down to the shore yet again and, ten minutes later, he returned, accompanied by a class three corpsman. Aboard the seaplane, the corpsman informed me, was a doctor waiting to see me. He would examine me on our way to the naval hospital. Ron asked the corpsman if it was okay if I ate something.

"Anything he wants," replied the corpsman, adding that after I had eaten, we would walk down to the plane.

After wolfing down two eggs Ron had cooked sunny side-up – man, they looked pretty as a picture I had thought when he set them before me, along with a steaming cup of coffee – I loved coffee, but this cup was so bitter and bad that I was unable to drink it – one problem still remained. Though all my blisters had dried, they had also begun to tighten and crack, and so I was still unable to straighten my legs due to the searing blasts of pain. In other words, I was unable to stand and walk down to the plane. Acknowledging this, the corpsman left and, about a half hour later, returned with two other Coast Guard corpsmen, both in their mid-twenties, though I cannot recall their rank. One was about my size, the other much bigger, about twice my size. As for Ron, from the perspective of my then twenty-year-old eyes, he looked elderly, but, in retrospect, now that I am seventy-five, I think he was probably middle-aged, probably around fifty.

Unable to stretch my legs and stand, let alone walk, the problem of how to transport me down to the seaplane was resolved with a bit of quick-thinking and ingenuity on Ron's part- certainly a key to survival for anyone living alone on Kodiak Island. After hooking up a flatbed trailer to his tractor, Ron pulled it up in front of his cabin. As I remained seated in the kitchen chair, the two corpsmen then hoisted me up and carried me – the saddest excuse ever of a king on his throne – to the back of the trailer. A corpsman on either side of me, like sentinels standing guard to make sure my "throne" did not tip over, Ron transported us down to a small cove along the beach. Once we arrived, the corpsmen lifted me up and placed me in a seat aboard a small aluminum motorboat. With the smaller of the two Coast Guardsmen behind me, controlling the motor, and the much bigger one up front, after bidding Ron a fond farewell and thank-you, we headed out into the channel to the seaplane, the name "Goose" inscribed on its side. Just as we arrived at the channel's end, however, about to enter choppy water, the first large wave we encountered inundated the boat. Drenched again, the frigid saltwater sent sharp stings up and down my legs and feet, threatening to turn my blisters back to open wounds. The boat completely flooded, but with the motor still running, we were forced to turn around and head to a narrow peninsula that extended out from the cove. Meanwhile, as he watched from shore, enjoying our misadventure, Ron smiled and then laughed.

Upon returning to land, none too pleased with what had happened, my blisters burning like bee stings and razor cuts, I sat as the two corpsmen got out and nearly tipped the boat over to empty the water. Struggling to remain upright in my seat, wincing in pain as I tried to avoid falling in the water, I barked, "What the hell you trying to do, drown me?"

Sometime later, the water emptied, to lighten our load and stay atop the waves, the bigger of the two corpsmen remained on shore while the other and I made a second attempt to get to the *Goose*, about 400 yards away. Finally, the motor humming as we skipped along atop the waves, we achieved success.

Once we arrived, with the motor idling, we slowly entered the back of the seaplane, directly between its two rows of seats. Those aboard the *Goose* then helped me out of the boat and onto a seat as the corpsman returned to shore to pick up his mate. Once everyone was back on board, the opening in the rear of the plane now closed and sealed, as we moved forward in the ocean, steadily accelerating, the water that had washed into the plane was quickly expelled. And suddenly we took off. What a rush! I was finally heading home!

About twenty minutes later, we touched down at the naval base. Feeling self-conscious, more than a little embarrassed, I saw that a small crowd of friends had gathered to welcome me back. Their broad smiles told me how happy they all were to see me, and that, against all odds, I had survived. Immediately several corpsmen placed me in a gurney and then rushed me by ambulance to an operating room at the naval hospital, where several doctors awaited my arrival. After summarily examining me, they suddenly burst into laughter. Their prognosis: I smelled and desperately needed a nice, warm bath, nourishment, and medication to heal my wounds. After bathing me, I was then given a general physical. The startling result was that during my plight, in which I travelled approximately seventy miles in a horseshoe pattern, I had lost thirty pounds and one-inch in height since my mustering-out physical administered on September 1.

A half-hour later, with an intravenous line in my arm for hydration, in a room outside the operating suite, a steady stream of friends and well-wishers came to visit me. Straight-faced, I told them that I was never really lost, that I always knew where I was.

"All I had to do was pick up my foot and mark the ground with an 'X,'" I joked. "That's exactly where I was. I just had no idea where all you guys were."

With that, we all enjoyed a good laugh, and soon I received orders to call home.

As it turned out, upon my arrival at the naval base, radio station WPOP in Hartford, Connecticut, which had established an open line to Kodiak after my Uncle Richard's phone call in response to its story-of-the-week contest, instantly announced that I had been found. That I was alive and well. Upon hearing the news, my mother, who had cried every day and night since hearing I was lost, and had rarely eaten or slept, cried yet again. Now, however, she shed tears of joy rather than pain. Moreover, the news effectively freed Uncle Richard from my parents' "doghouse." Concerning his phone call in response to the radio station's contest, all was forgiven.

My call home that night lasted approximately twenty minutes, at a cost of about $80.00. Back in 1964, that was a lot of money, the equivalent of about $665.00 today. Since they had already heard WPOP's announcement, simply hearing my voice brought further incredible joy to my parents and everyone else in my family. Suddenly, in all their eyes, I had become even more special, a local hero. All my uncles were immensely proud of me – overly proud – especially Uncle George, and even Uncle Freddy, who, though he had shunned me when I was a kid, immediately became one of my biggest fans. From then on, he always wanted me to travel to Maine with him, so he could brag to everyone there about my overcoming the odds and surviving lost and alone on Kodiak Island- while encountering, of course, the island's giant brown bears. As time passed, however, I would always refuse to go. He had never taken me when I was a kid, when I could have used his attention and example of how a good uncle should act – how any loving, caring adult should act- so why would I want to accompany him now? No way was I about to grant Uncle Freddy bragging rights concerning me- not now, not ever. Years later, however, I would grow to love the old buzzard and, because he was a glazier *par excellence*, I would even hire him to work with me in my plate glass business.

Finally, in a telegram to my parents sent on this day, Vice Admiral Semmes stated that he was "…pleased to confirm on behalf of the United States Navy that your son, Joseph Bruce LaChance, previously reported missing was found…at a ranch house at Saltery Cove, Alaska…." And that though I was admitted to the station hospital for recuperation, "I had not been injured…"

As it also turned out, along with becoming an instant hero to everyone back home, I had also impressed the Navy with my successful battle to survive. In the ensuing days, however, much of the Navy's initial impression would devolve into anger and controversy regarding my actions. More than 100 men had participated in the six-day search for me and, for that, and other reasons, which I shall detail shortly, some in high command felt I should pay a stiff price. A very stiff price.

WESTERN UNION

TELEGRAM

W. P. MARSHALL, PRESIDENT

The filing time shown in the date line on domestic telegrams is STANDARD TIME at point of origin. Time of receipt is STANDARD TIME at point of destination

BB195   Duplicate of Telephoned (27)

B SGA255 RX GOVT PD TDSG PWS ARLINGTON VIR 23 1128A EDT

MR AND MRS JOSEPH AMBROSE LACHANCE

46 SECRET LAKE RD AVON CONN

I AM PLEASED TO CONFIRM ON BEHALF OF THE UNITED STATES NAVY THAT

YOUR SON, JOSEPH BRUCE LACHANCE   PREVIOUSLY REPORTED MISSING WAS

FOUND ON 22 SEPTEMBER 1964   AT A RANCH HOUSE AT SALTERY COVE ALASKA

YOUR SON IS NOT INJURED   BUT HAS BEEN ADMITTED TO THE STATION

HOSPITAL FOR RECUPERATION.

    VICE ADMIRAL B J SEMMES JR CHIEF OF NAVAL PERSONNEL

BUPERS

THE FALLOUT

IN THE DAYS following my rescue and return to the station – much of which is now a blur – an array of friends continued to visit me in the hospital as I recuperated. Often when we talked, they would ask, "What was it like to be lost?" And I would respond with my "X" on the ground routine that we all thought was funny. On the 24th, one friend even brought me a cupcake with a candle in it- for my twenty-first birthday. The following day, after having been interviewed by a reporter, a story recounting my "adventure" appeared in the naval station's newspaper, the *Kodiak Bear*. I was becoming quite a celebrity.

When Chase arrived for a visit, he filled me in on what he and Arthur Cook had done in search of me, along with the other ground and air search parties. Of course, he made it a point to let me know about the helicopter he had boarded after miraculously discovering my trail with the number "7" in my footprints; and how the copter, even at full throttle, refused to rise simply due to his weight being added to that of the others already on board. We both laughed at this, along with what the pilot had said: "If this guy finds his way out of the woods,

I'm going to kick his ass." As it turned out, the pilot, Lt. Paul Wheeler, also came to visit me and, after thanking him, I did offer to get out of bed and let him boot my ass. Thankfully, he declined and, instead, he offered me this advice before leaving: "Bruce, you need to stop saying you were never lost. That you always knew where you were. And stop making that 'X' on the floor. It isn't a joke. You need to stop." As I was about to learn, someone much higher in rank than Lt. Wheeler more than agreed. And he intended to do something about it.

On September 25 or 26 – as I have said, much of this is a blur – Chief Pearson came to see me. I was happy he did. He had been my first chief commander, up until August 1, and I had grown to admire him both as an officer and a man. As I quickly realized, however, Chief Pearson had paid a visit not only to see how I was and tell me how glad he felt that I was alive, but to repeat Lt. Wheeler's warning to stop treating what I had done as a joke.

"Captain Gee wants to throw the book at you," he cautioned me, as if I had deliberately gone AWOL. Captain Gee's official title was U.S. Navy Commanding Officer, U.S. Naval Station, Kodiak, Alaska. "He wants to hang your ass," Chief Pearson continued. "He wants you to remain in the service until you pay back all the cost in man hours and flight time it took searching for you. He thinks you went AWOL on purpose because you keep saying you knew where you were all along. Stop with your joking, Bruce!"

Realizing the trouble I had gotten myself in, though I was angry and felt wrongly accused, I heeded the advice offered by Lt. Wheeler and Chief Pearson. As the sobering truth sank in, and the possible ramifications it held for me, I knew they were right. None of what I had done and experienced was a joke.

As it turned out, over the next few days, while still hospitalized, I began to hear other things, some fact, some mere rumors. It was a fact, as Chief Pearson had also informed me while visiting, that the admiral at the naval station had no desire to punish me. That he was at odds with Captain Gee over the entire issue of my being deliberately

AWOL. And that Captain Gee – this information was hearsay – had told the admiral the day before my twenty-first birthday, "He's not even a man yet. He's only twenty. He needs to learn a lesson."

According to the story, the admiral replied to Captain Gee, "You will do nothing to that man. LaChance is more of a man than a whole bunch of older personnel."

At least, I thought, I had the admiral's support. I had served faithfully under him, to the best of my ability, for eighteen months. Now, however, I wondered how far my dedication to both him and the Navy would go in determining my fate. And if my scheduled discharge would be delayed if Captain Gee had his way. And for how long.

On the 27th or 28th of September, I learned my Captain's Mast was scheduled for the morning of October 1. I would find out then the answers to all my questions. Everything was up to Captain Gee. My fate was in his hands.

Captain's Mast is the Navy term for Non-Judicial Punishment (NJP). The term is applied when a sailor is in violation of the Uniform Code of Military Justice (UCMJ), and it is defined as the "non-judicial punishment of an enlisted person by a military commanding officer." As the term "non-judicial" implies, a Captain's Mast is not a trial. Rather, it is a procedure whereby the commanding officer (CO), in my case, Captain R.P. Gee, must dispose of any charges either by dismissing them, imposing punishment under the provisions of military law, or referring the case to a court-martial. Should the commanding officer decide to impose punishment, again, according to military law, the CO has five different sentences from which to choose:

- Admonition or reprimand;
- Confinement on bread and water/diminished rations: not more than three days and only on grades E-3 and below attached to or embarked in a vessel (USN and USMC only);

- Correctional custody: not more than seven days;
- Forfeiture: not more than seven days' pay;
- Reduction: to next inferior pay grade on E-7 and above (Navy, Army, and Air Force) or E-6 and above (Marine Corps), if rank from which demoted is within the promotion authority of the Officer in Command.

In arriving at his final decision, Captain Gee considered the following factors, which he detailed in an official Letter of Reprimand, handed to me during my Captain's Mast on the morning of October 1. He summarized the same information in a letter to my parents, which he sent the following day.

"You were absent without leave from 0745, 17 September 1964 until 1100, 22 September 1964…Against all good practice, went alone into the wilderness of Sharatin Bay, Kodiak Island without a compass, map, or sleeping bag, all of which contributed to your becoming lost and ultimately to your unauthorized absence…and the organization of an extensive search which lasted five days and required 1,078 man hours of the ground search parties, 26 flight hours of a helicopter, 15 flight hours of an amphibious aircraft, and four days of time by the station tug boat. You, lost but fortunately unhurt, now failed to stay in one place or to make signals to aid the searchers. Instead, you kept constantly on the move, traveling from Sharatin Bay to Kizhuyak Bay and through a 2,200 foot mountain pass into Ugak Bay, a distance of almost 50 miles…On the morning of 22 September 1964, by good fortune and a lucky turn, you stumbled upon the home of a rancher. Your condition required hospital care, and you had been on unauthorized absence for five days."

In the end, based on these facts, and with the admiral's backing, Captain Gee thus issued me the lightest scolding possible – a letter of reprimand – for what he finally determined was an offense of minor nature. What a break! And as Captain Gee concluded in his letter to my parents, "I am personally pleased that all turned out well and that

IN REPLY REFER TO:
LE
1620

OCT 1 1964

FOR OFFICIAL USE ONLY

From: Commanding Officer, U. S. Naval Station, Kodiak, Alaska
To: LaCHANCE, Joseph B., 595 92 21, RM3, USN

Subj: Letter of reprimand

Ref: (a) Article 15, UCMJ
        (b) JAG Manual Section 0102

1. In accordance with reference (a) and (b), this letter is addressed to you as punishment awarded you at Captain's Mast.

2. You were granted leave from 0001 hours 1 September 1964 until 0745 hours 17 September 1964. On 17 September when you failed to report off leave, command was informed you had not returned from a hunting trip into the wilderness of Sharatin Bay, Kodiak Island. Command was further informed that against all good practice, you had gone alone and without a compass, map or sleeping bag. An extensive search was organized. This search lasted five days and required 1,078 man hours of the ground search parties, 26 flight hours of a helicopter, 15 flight hours of an amphibious aircraft, and four days of time by the station tug boat. You, lost but fortunately unhurt, now failed to stay in one place or to make signals to aid the searchers. Instead you kept constantly on the move, traveling from Sharatin Bay to Kizhuyak Bay and through a 2,200 foot mountain pass into Ugak Bay, a distance of almost 50 miles. You were several days ahead of the pursuing search party of trackers when, on the morning of 22 September 1964, by good fortune and a lucky turn, you stumbled upon the home of a rancher. Your condition required hospital care, and you had been on unauthorized absence for five days.

3. Under the circumstances, you neglected your duties to the United States Navy in that you:

    a. Were absent without leave from your organization from 0745, 17 September 1964 until 1100, 22 September 1964.

    b. Went into the Alaskan wilderness of Sharatin Bay, without a companion or compass, which is strictly against good practice of safety in the wilderness. This lack of compass and companion contributed to your becoming lost and ultimately to your unauthorized absence.

    c. Once lost, failed to remain in one place making signs to aid rescuers, but instead kept constantly on the move leaving an arduous trail for searchers to follow. This behavior increased the amount of time absent.

FOR OFFICIAL USE ONLY

FOR OFFICIAL USE ONLY

4. You are hereby reprimanded for your derelictions and unauthorized absence as set forth in the preceding paragraph.

5. You are hereby advised of your right to appeal this action to the next superior authority, Commandant, Seventeenth Naval District, in accordance with the provisions of Article 15(e) of the Uniform Code of Military Justice, paragraph 135 of the Manual for Courts-Martial, United States, 1951, and Section 0102f. of the Manual of the Judge Advocate General.

6. If, upon full consideration, you do not desire to avail yourself of this right to appeal, you are directed so to inform the Chief of Naval Personnel through official channels. You are directed to reply without delay, through official channels, and to state therein the date of receipt of this communication, and the approximate time when either an appeal or notice of decision not to appeal may be expected. Any subsequent request for additional time shall contain adequate justification therefore.

7. Unless withdrawn, or set aside by higher authority, a copy of this letter will be placed in your official record in the Bureau of Naval Personnel. You are therefore privileged to forward within fifteen days after receipt of final determination of your appeal or after the date of your notification of your decision not to appeal, whichever may be applicable, such statement concerning this letter as you may desire, also for inclusion in your record. If you elect not to submit a statement, you shall state so officially in writing within the time above prescribed. In connection with your statement, attention is directed to Articles 1404.2 and 3, U. S. Navy Regulations, 1948.

R. P. Lee

Joseph is back with us in excellent health to continue to serve his country as an excellent citizen and U.S. Naval Reservist."

After handing me my letter of reprimand and reading it aloud, Captain Gee twice asked me if I wanted to disagree with the reprimand in any way. Though I inwardly disagreed with some of its wording, both times I replied, "No, sir." And then close to concluding, Captain Gee issued me my final punishment. I was to go on television with Ovid McKinley and explain why no one should ever go hunting alone; why a hunting plan should always be filed; and why no one should ever take the actions I had, both before and while journeying into the wilderness, that had made it nearly impossible for ground and air search parties to find me.

Attired in my dress blues, I had been nervous both before and throughout my Captain's Mast. And then as I finally began to relax a bit, Captain Gee concluded by informing me, "We have one more thing to do." With that, we stood, stepped outside his office, and then outside the building. Where fifty of the men who had taken part in the five-day search now stood, arranged in such a way as to spell out "KODIAK." Nearly overwhelmed with surprise, more grateful than ever, accompanied by Captain Gee, the naval station's admiral, Ovid McKinley, and David Henley, I positioned myself with them in front as a photographer atop the building I worked in snapped our picture. But only after I had thanked everyone and apologized for what I had put them through. Of course, I knew some of the men, others I was meeting for the first time. Feeling more self-conscious than ever, I let them all know how touched I was and that I owed each a debt of gratitude.

Once the "ceremony" concluded, Ovid McKinley gave me a ride back to my barracks, where I now lived rather than with Chase and Edie and their kids. That way, we had decided, Ovid would know where to pick me up later that night, or the next, depending on when our television appearance would be scheduled. As part of my preparation, I had decided to make a large map detailing where I had travelled

each day of my journey. I would bring the map with me as a visual aid on the show.

Along the way to the barracks, Ovid and I discussed what we were going to say on the live broadcast. Most specifically, we discussed an issue Captain Gee had raised in my letter of reprimand- the dangers and irresponsibility of going hunting alone, without filing a plan to guide others in case something went wrong, such as getting lost. I reminded Ovid that it was he who had told me to "never go hunting with someone you cannot trust, that you're better to go alone," so you would keep your cool and take necessary precautions before firing at your prey. Something the hunting partner you could not trust might not do- with deadly results, both for him and you. Upon my mentioning this, immediately Ovid, with a deadly serious look in his eye, responded, "If you tell anyone that, I will kill you." Unbeknownst to me at the time, Ovid's job as head of Alaska's Department of Fish and Game, as well as David Henley's, had begun just a year ago, and if I announced his warning on TV, surely both he and Henley would be fired. In response to Ovid's threat and menacing glare, I merely smiled, but in the hours leading up to the broadcast, which would take place that night, we later learned, his words only added fuel to my nervousness and fear about appearing on live television. Considering all that I had just been through in my struggle to survive – barely survive – I found it ironic that I now felt so overwhelmed by such a comparatively small matter as appearing on TV. Such, I suppose, is the power of self-consciousness, and our fear of others' judgments, even if we suppose ourselves infallible, as I still did.

In 1964, the only television programming available on Kodiak was broadcast from the naval base, which had a signal radius of twenty miles. Located seven miles east of the base, the town of Kodiak, itself, with a population of about 3,200 – minus the fifteen that had been killed as a result of a tectonic tsunami that struck it during the March earthquake – lay well within the signal's radius. Thus, at the time of our broadcast, Kodiak was still recovering from the deaths and $11 million worth of destruction caused by the thirty-foot waves. The tsunami had wiped out the neighboring Native villages of Old Harbor and Kaguyak. The Standard Oil Company, the Alaskan King Crab Company, and much of the fishing fleet had also been destroyed by the tsunami- a result of the strongest earthquake ever recorded in North America. Kodiak was also where most married members of the Navy, Marines, and Coast Guard lived with their families. None had perished during the quake and tsunami that year. So, it was against this background that I was about to make my television debut, with most of Kodiak watching.

Having appeared on TV before, after picking me up at 6:30 p.m., Ovid did his best to calm my fears. Empathetic, understanding my apprehension about appearing on television, he made no further threats. We both wanted things to go smoothly.

When we finally arrived about ten minutes early at the station, a nondescript building, to say the least, and went inside, the TV crew quickly took my map and placed it on a tripod before the camera. After the production supervisor seated Ovid and me at small tables adjacent to one another, with the map to my left, he then began the countdown to airtime. "Three…Two…One…You're on."

Oh, shit! That was my first thought as the camera's red light came on. And then I relaxed a bit, breathed a sigh of relief as I noticed the camera was focused solely on Ovid.

After introducing first himself and then me – *Calm down, Bruce… Calm down* – Ovid then continued, "We are here tonight to talk about safe hunting, and the importance of filing a ground plan prior to going off on any hunting trip, especially on Kodiak."

A brief question and answer session regarding those conjoined topics then ensued, with Ovid asking all the questions, while adding his expertise to my responses. Finally, Ovid asked me to discuss in detail my ten-day ordeal. While referring to the map I had made, I described every place I had stopped for the night and my daily experiences, especially my encounters with Kodiak bears. With the camera often focused on the map – much to my relief – the time passed quickly, and soon our allotted half-hour had nearly expired. Just before it did, Ovid turned directly to me and said, "So, Joe, the final message for our viewers is to always let people know your hunting plan, start to finish, and never go alone. Isn't that right?"

On cue, and as Ovid had cautioned me to respond, I answered, "Yes. Plan for anything that might happen. Always file a ground plan. And *never* go alone."

With that, the show ended. And Ovid still had his job.

In the ensuing days, my last ever on Kodiak, my new "celebrity" status served to both renew and inflate my sense of infallibility. The Rosary that I had clung to and the prayers that I had said to help me through my plight? Seldom did I think of them now, and seldom did I pray. Everywhere I went, people, especially children, whispered and pointed at me in awe and admiration- the young man, the hero, who had miraculously survived ten days lost and alone, near starvation, on Kodiak Island. No one else had ever come close to doing such a thing- what had been considered impossible. A miracle, indeed.

Both proud and self-conscious, on October 3 or 4, I no longer remember which, I was on my way back to Connecticut. Home. And a whole new adventure. One that would also involve miracles, while, again, lost and found. Not in Alaska. Not on Kodiak. But in a dark place in my life. A place where many of us perish, and few survive.

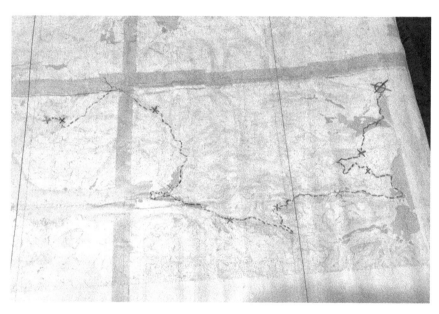

This map shows where I slept each night when I was lost.

PART THREE
LOST AGAIN

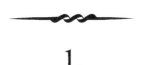

1.

ON OCTOBER 3 or 4 – again, I no longer recall which – I boarded a plane in Kodiak bound for Seattle. From there, I would fly to Chicago, for a connector flight to what is now Bradley International Airport, just outside Hartford, Connecticut. And close to home.

What I clearly recall about my trip home is that I bought a beer at the airport in Chicago while awaiting my flight to Hartford. Having just turned twenty-one, and because I still looked underage, I was carded. After examining my driver's license, the bartender finally looked up at me, smiled and said, "Happy birthday!' As it turned out, I did not enjoy the beer. I had bought it only because I could: I was twenty-one; I was an adult. I was a man. As the years passed, however, and the legal drinking age in Connecticut was lowered to eighteen, because I continued to look much younger than my age, I was almost always carded. That finally ended when I turned twenty-eight.

As I awaited my ride home from Bradley to Avon – I cannot recall who eventually picked me up – I began to feel uncomfortable. Self-conscious. I had been treated as a hero in Kodiak and been written about in newspapers. But how would I be treated by friends and family once I arrived home? As a hero, of course. I had no desire, however, to be the center of anyone's attention, in any way. The last thing I wanted was to make a big deal out of anything, especially myself, and what I had experienced while lost and alone on Kodiak Island. But others either could not, or would not, see it that way. Once back home, I discovered that seemingly overnight, I had become everyone's hero, a "big shot" not only in Avon, my hometown, but the entire state of Connecticut. James V. Healion, a reporter for United Press International, interviewed me and, on October 21 and 22, my story and photo appeared in newspapers nationwide. Connecticut newspapers, including *The Hartford Times*, the *Hartford Courant*, and the *New Britain Herald*, also carried my story and photo. In his first of two dispatches, Healion wrote, "Survival experts say some men roll with the punches in an emergency, while others disintegrate into psychic shambles." I, of course, was the former, the man who had never panicked, who had overcome the odds against survival, the man who had defied nature and death. And yes, I continued to believe I was infallible, that the world and life itself were all about me. The Rosary I had carried with me and used to pray for God's help? I never thought about those prayer beads, anymore. I no longer knew where they were, almost as if they had never existed, as if they had played little, if any, role in my survival.

With all that said, ironically, however, I took no enjoyment in my newly found fame. Though suddenly, it seemed, everyone wanted to be my friend and hang out with me, I continued to view myself and my Alaska "experience" as no big deal. I had gotten lost in the wilderness for ten days mostly due to my own negligence, and I had been reprimanded for it. Moreover, it was only because Chase, in a "God moment," had discovered that number "7" in my tracks that the search parties knew what direction I was heading and that I was still alive. And that was why Ron Hurst already knew who I was before welcoming me into his home. Maybe due to ten days of "God moments," I had found my way to his cabin in the woods. In hindsight, I guess, in a way, I was experiencing how myths and legends are created, and that this small-town boy was, at least for now, becoming one of those myths. Shortly after Healion's story about me, accompanied by my photo, appeared nationwide, I began to receive a lot of mail. In one letter, a young reader congratulated me not for defying the odds and surviving, but for simply getting my name in the newspaper. He explained to me that the only way he could have gotten his name in the paper was if he had shot someone. I received mail from all over the country, from as far away as California. I guess in today's parlance, you might say that overnight, I was becoming both a legend and a "rock star."

When I was released from the naval hospital, I was instructed not to do anything for a month, so, despite my growing notoriety, I tried my best to relax and enjoy my family and friends again. The day after I arrived home to a hero's welcome, a former high school girlfriend named Donna called. We had dated right up until the day I enlisted in the Navy. While in Radioman School, however, she sent me a "Dear John" letter to let me know she was ending our relationship. During her phone call, Donna said she had heard about me on WPOP when the radio station announced my uncle Richard had won the $14.10 for submitting the week's winning news story. She then asked if I would like to go out with her.

I did go on that date with Donna and oh, did I fall head over heels for her again! No doubt about it, I decided, she was the one for me, and we continued dating over the next fourteen months. At the risk of getting too far ahead of myself – perhaps, way too far – I'll tell you about those fourteen months now. After all, they would prove to be both an omen and the seed of things to come- of my downward spiral into the *disease* of alcoholism, where, again, there is no map or compass to guide you out of the wilderness – its wilderness – and where, without realizing it, day by day, you just start falling to the bottom of the barrel. Until you finally hit rock bottom, however deep that may be, and you use that moment and the "crash" to awaken yourself. Resurrect yourself. And live again. Unless, of course, you never hit bottom, and the disease kills you instead. And death was your rock bottom....

While dating Donna again, I got to meet everyone in her family – parents, big brother, and younger sister Sally, or "Annabanana," as I called her. Donna's uncle Chick was the business agent for the local glazier's union, and I got to meet him, as well. I had grown up in an extended family of glaziers – uncles George and Freddie and cousin Little Freddie were all glaziers – so I was familiar with the trade, and it appealed to me as a possible career choice. Uncle George agreed with me, and he encouraged me to pursue it. They all made good money, and Little Freddie even drove a new car. Why not me, too? I thought, and Uncle George again agreed, promising to help me any way he could- but on one condition: that Pittsburgh Plate Glass, located in Connecticut, despite its name, had a slot open for a glazier's apprentice. George firmly believed PPG would be the best place for me, as it would also offer me a good education. Furthermore, he and Chick were already friends. I promised him I would ask Chick ASAP if there was an opening.

One day, when Donna and I were out together, we stopped in at Chick and his wife Dala's house for a visit. There, I was amazed to see, for the very first time, a color TV. *The Flintstones*, a new cartoon show, was on. My, I thought, how life had changed in just three years, from 1961, when I entered the service, until now, 1964. Seemingly everything had changed, especially the cars. Already, companies were pushing their new '65 models, and they were impressive.

That day, armed with what Uncle George had said, bolstered by his belief in me and what I had promised him in return, I asked Chick if there was an apprentice opening at PPG. And if there was one, I told him that I wanted a shot at it. Chick promised he would gladly check into it for me.

Chick and Uncle George golfed together every Saturday, but unknown to George, was that Chick was my girlfriend Donna's uncle. While out golfing one Saturday, George asked Chick if PPG had an apprentice slot open, and then he explained that he wanted a nephew of his, meaning me, of course, to get it. He did not mention me by name or provide any further information. Chick replied that there was indeed an opening, but he already had someone to fill it- his niece's boyfriend, again, of course, meaning me. Instantly George erupted.

"I'm talking about my nephew, Chick! A blood relation. And you're going to fill the spot with your niece's boyfriend? Over my dead body! I'll kick your ass if you do! You wait till you bring your choice up on the floor. You won't be the union's business agent after that meeting!"

Having no idea what had occurred between the two men, one day I decided to visit Uncle George. He happened to mention Chick's name and I said I knew him. That he was my girlfriend Donna's uncle. Suddenly realizing what had happened, that he and Chick had no quarrel because they both wanted me to fill the opening, Uncle George burst out laughing. I guess, like the others in my family, I was meant to be a glazier, and on November 19, 1964, I spent my first day as an apprentice at PPG. Soon after that, a local television station interviewed me regarding my Kodiak adventure while I was at work. I was in the middle of helping another employee move large aluminum window frames we were fabricating for a seven-story building when the interviewer appeared. This time, not only did I feel embarrassed by my notoriety, I felt guilty about it, because I was taking time away from my new job to talk to these television people. It was wrong, I thought, and I felt selfish.

I loved my trade, the skills it involved, and the people I worked with. Prior to my first day, George – it feels funny to call my uncle George just plain "George," as I had called him "Uncle George" until the day he died in 2017 – had cautioned me that if I established a bad reputation for myself, it would stay with me for the remainder of my life. That it could not be changed to a good one, but a good reputation could turn into a bad one. "Good is always better," he concluded, so

I had remembered his warning on the day of the TV interview, and hoped I had not done myself a life-long disservice due to selfishness.

As it turned out, I hadn't. Nor would it take me long to make to establish a good reputation. I learned fast and eagerly, and soon everyone wanted me to work with them. Furthermore, Chick said he would give me "top billing" with Donna's family. Life was suddenly all good. And I was still infallible.

On December 16, 1965, Donna turned twenty-one and, as a gift, I gave her a hope chest. I also planned to ask her to marry me on Christmas Day. I had bought a diamond ring at Bill Savitt's famous Hartford jewelry store, where every purchase came with a "POMG," a "Peace of Mind Guarantee." Every Wednesday, my pay day, I would stop by the store to make a payment on the layaway plan I had agreed to. That is, until things went awry.

A day or two after Donna's birthday, I stopped by her house to see her. Her mother told me she wasn't home, but she invited me in, and we talked for about half an hour. I told her about my plan to ask Donna to marry me on Christmas Day. She asked that I wait instead. I replied that I was still going to ask her, but that we would wait awhile before we got married.

Then Donna's father arrived home. Immediately her mom got up from her chair and said, "I would like you to ask Bruce to leave. He has been rude and very disrespectful to me."

"That's not true," I politely disagreed. "I haven't been disrespectful or rude." Apparently, I thought, her mom had misunderstood me.

Of course, you know who won that argument, and as I left, Donna arrived. I told her that her mom was not telling the truth and I would call her in the morning. When I did, her father answered, but Donna picked up on another phone and said, "I got this, dad," and he hung up. Then she told me the crushing news.

"I can't see you anymore."

"What? You can't mean that!" I replied, my world suddenly in chaos.

"I can't see you anymore," she repeated.

And that was that. There was no going back. I never spoke to Donna again.

On the Wednesday before Christmas, on the 22nd, I walked broken-hearted into Bill Savitt's to make what was supposed to be my final payment. As I arrived at the counter, the salesman, who was familiar with me, greeted me with, "Hi, Bruce. Let me get your ring."

"Nope," I muttered, and feeling emptier than ever, I shook my head.

Stopping dead in his tracks, he turned back to face me and asked, "What?"

"I said no." Again, I shook my head. "I want my money back."

"What happened, Bruce?" he asked, both shocked and puzzled.

"She broke up with me," I explained, wishing to leave it at that. "So I want my money back. I have a 'POMG.'"

Of course, speaking both literally and figuratively, nothing could have been further from the truth. My mind was shattered, and so was my heart. Thankfully, however, the salesman complied, and he returned my money.

I cried for two days after my final trip to the jewelry store, and then I started drinking. Heavily. I drank for much of the next three years, nearly every day and night, while racing stock cars, carousing, and drinking more and more. I never really got drunk, however, no stumbling around or falling. Nothing like that. But I did have many blackouts. Miraculously, I drove through them without ever having an accident and, perhaps, those, too, were "God moments" in my life. I wasn't meant to die then, and neither was anyone else due to my drinking.

Haunted by Donna's breaking up with me, I drank heavily the following Christmas and New Year's, as well as at every party I attended and on any other occasion when the opportunity presented itself. Along the way, I was welcomed everywhere I went, and I made many new friends, but none of them could ever replace Donna or mend my broken heart. My celebrity status was still working, and though I continued to bask in the limelight, often self-medicated with alcohol, sometimes, as I have said, I found the whole situation, as well as life, totally incomprehensible. I deserved none of the notoriety, I thought, because, again, I had done nothing special, accomplished nothing deserving of such attention and praise.

Looking back on everything, I think it is safe to say that clearly, though I may not have realized it, I was at war with myself.

By the spring of 1966, however, I had filled my life with many new people, activities, and interests, including the Farmington River Water Ski Club, and I had also continued racing stock cars, which would consume much of my life for the next three years. During that time, a friend named Mac McDonald and I became race car partners, while "Vinny," his previous partner, slowly faded from the scene, though we all remained friends. I was not a very good driver, but every week I showed signs of improvement, and so there was hope for me in our racing endeavors. Mac and I raced every Saturday night at Riverside Park in Agawam, Massachusetts, a well-known venue for stock car racing, and then spend the following week repairing any damage to the car so we could race again the following Saturday. By the end of our initial year of racing and repairing, Mac and I both had become better drivers and, as a result, the next season, needing to make far fewer repairs, we improved our finishes mostly through tune-ups and minor adjustments.

Mac and I worked constantly on our car, except on Thursdays, which we spent at the Polish Club in Hartford, where we soon became a fixture. Though consumed with racing, I was also consuming alcohol on a daily basis- beer when working on the car, Seagram's Seven and Seven-Up, or crème de menthe on the rocks, when I was out with friends. At the Polish Club, I got to know the bartender pretty well, and when I felt I had had enough, or, if feeling that way and someone wanted to buy me a drink, I would tell him to pour me some ginger ale instead. To that extent, and at this point in my life, I did have my drinking "under control," but even that failed to prevent me from making the long drive home to Avon amid blackouts, always coming to just before turning left onto my street, Secret Lake Road. Again, looking back, it seems miraculous that I never killed myself or anyone else in an accident, "God moments," too, in their own way.

While all this was going on, Vinny's girlfriend, Carol, fixed me up with one of her co-workers. Her name was Maribeth, and in 1968, after dating for about a year, we decided to get married. Maribeth and I were living in an apartment in East Hartford, and one evening Carol and Vinny came over to visit. While the "girls" sat in the living room, Vinny and I sat at the kitchen table downing the quart of Seagram's Seven he had brought with him. As we drank, eventually I realized that due to the whiskey, I was telling Vinny the same story I had already repeated to him three or four times, and that for the same reason, he was also repeating himself to me. As a result, I paid more attention to how much I drank and became more careful to avoid overdoing it.

Soon after that night, another "incident" involving alcohol, one much more extreme, not only snared my attention, it had a downright sobering effect on me. One night, Maribeth's father got so drunk he crashed face-first on his kitchen floor and passed out. All night, he lay there in a pool of blood. When Maribeth and I arrived the following evening for dinner, her father greeted us with two black eyes. I was so shocked and disgusted, even sickened, I decided to stop drinking- at least for a while. There was no way I wanted the same thing, or anything similar, to happen to me. Neither Maribeth nor I drank much after that evening. In fact, later that same year, at Christmas, because we had company coming over to our apartment, I bought a case of Miller High Life Lite beer. Maribeth and I drank very little of it and, a year later, some of it still sat unopened in our refrigerator. The image of her father's battered face, as if he had been severely beaten, just would not go away.

Shortly before Maribeth and I went on our honeymoon, I completed my apprenticeship and was asked to work "inside" for PPG's contract sales. Although I was an excellent mechanic and glazier, I agreed to become an estimator, buying and selling jobs and computing their costs. Returning to work after our honeymoon, I now wore a suit and tie at work, but, as it turned out, it soon became obvious that I was a much better glazier than a salesman. Selling just wasn't in me. It wasn't me. And I didn't enjoy it nearly as much as the "hands-on" nature of a glazier's job.

During the first three years of our marriage, Maribeth and I tried to have children, but with no success. Eventually, as a result of medical tests, we learned that I had an extremely low sperm count, which accounted for our "problem" with having children. In 1972, frustrated with our failure, we decided to adopt and, through the Catholic Charities organization, on September 23, we officially became our new son Jason's parents. It was also the day before my birthday, and I could not have received a better gift than Jason, who had been born on August 25, 1972.

Later in the year, now with a son to care for, when it came time for my performance review at PPG, I decided to ask for the maximum 10% raise. In response, my supervisor offered the minimum 4%, a raise much smaller than the ones I had received the previous two years. Angry and insulted, as I came to a slow boil, I decided then and there that I had had enough.

"You've been doing this kind of work a lot longer than I have," I responded to my boss and his measly offer. "I think I'm doing a good job, and I want and deserve ten percent. But you think I'm doing a bad job. You're entitled to your opinion, and I'll accept it. But I'm going back to working as a glazier. We both know I'm good at that."

In response, my boss offered me another job- working with Stan, the best man at my wedding. I said that I would think about it, but when I told Stan about the offer, he explained there was not enough work for the two of us, and one of us would eventually be shown the door, most likely, him. I would then be working alone, at a much lower pay rate. In the end, seeking to do what I felt was best for me and my family, I decided to return to my glazier's job and, six months later, I returned to see the doctor regarding my "problem." Suddenly my sperm count was through the roof. The doctor and I were both stunned.

"What's changed in your life?" he asked. "Did you change your job? Buy a house? Get a girlfriend?"

Immediately I replied, "I changed jobs," and to that, the doctor noted, "Don't you ever go back to a job like your old one. Keep the one you have now, and you'll do fine with trying to have a child."

Thus, in the end, my sperm count "dilemma" boiled down to one thing only: stress from a job that I did not enjoy, one that offered me little, if any, fulfillment, or even the most remote sense of accomplishment. Then and there I learned that stress can have all kinds of ill effects on one's life, ones that might even never occur to us. Like sperm count.

In January 1975, while working on my tax returns for the previous year, I saw that I had made $15,000. Later that month, on the 15th, just after the new Civic Center in downtown Hartford had been completed, I received notice that I had been laid off. In the first two weeks of 1975, I had already made $1,500, so I called the union hall seeking work. I was told that I was seventeenth on the waiting list and, with that in mind, calculating it was no big deal because I would be back at work soon, Maribeth and I decided to go on vacation for two weeks. But when we returned from vacation and I called the union again, I learned I was still seventeenth in line and that of the thirty-five other workers who had been laid off, so far none had been called back. Financially, things suddenly started to look bleak indeed.

In retrospect, however, though the union had no immediate or long-term plans for me, God did. On April 1, 1975, I opened my own glass shop. My unemployment pay was due to expire in July, so I continued to collect until then, when I would finally get my business off the ground. Everything seemed to be working out fine, until one day when I found myself waiting in line to collect- along with one of my new customers. That situation brought an abrupt end to my unemployment compensation, but by tax time, my business had already made $7,500, and I was feeling optimistic that my venture just might work. Other things, however, had begun to break down. Such as marriage. Despite our daughter Danielle's birth on July 13,1975, Maribeth and I stood on shaky ground. We both had hoped Danielle's birth would fix things, and that our family of four would stand as one. But it wasn't meant to be and, in 1976, after my dad had passed away on June 28, I decided to get a divorce. I not only blamed the collapse of our marriage on Maribeth's chronic and constant "crabbiness," but on my mother's also. Her incessant griping, I felt, had stretched my dad's ill health to the point of no return. In other words, I blamed her for my dad's death, which, as I look back, was simply untrue. But for me, at the time, it was. The grief and stress she had caused him, I was convinced, hammered the final nails into his coffin.

In August 1977 I finally moved out of the house and into a camper I kept at my glass shop. The following year, in September, my mother decided to move from Tolland, Connecticut, where she had been living since my father's death, to Colchester. One night after work, I showed up at the old house, along with my sister Sandy and her husband Mel, to help my mother clean. Since I had a dumpster at my business, I decided I would take everything there that she had decided to throw out. At one point, as Sandy, Mel, and I were talking in the garage, my mother appeared. She was carrying a set of rosary beads.

"Here's the rosary you had when you were lost, Bruce," she said, about to hand me the beads.

"Mom, these aren't mine," I impatiently replied, already angry because Mel wouldn't stop going through some of my dad's old things.

"God damn you, Bruce!" my mother exploded. "Just take them!" She placed the rosary in my hand. In turn, I tossed the beads, which I finally acknowledged to myself were the ones I had used to pray for God's help while lost, into a box of junk, which I then loaded into my van. As I have said, everything was about me.

The following day, when I arrived at my shop, I emptied all the boxes from my van into the dumpster, and then drove off to a job I had lined up. At day's end, however, when I arrived back at my shop and drove close to the dumpster, I saw the beads dangling from one of its bent edges near the opening. The crucified figure of Jesus was gone, along with the horizontal part of his cross.

"I don't think I was supposed to throw these away," I thought aloud, taking the beads from the dumpster's door, placing them instead on my rearview mirror, where they would remain for the next sixteen years, until 1994, when I removed them and placed them in my pocket. I have carried them with me now every day for twenty-five years. Ever since my first day in recovery, when I *knew* I was never supposed to have thrown them away. Another "God moment" along life's road, one that I will discuss in detail very shortly.

In November 1977, I moved in with a woman named Susan, along with her five kids, aged fifteen, fourteen, and nine, plus her eight-year-old twins. Maribeth and I had divorced in 1978, and on May 8, 1979 Susan and I married- but only after our son Joe had been born on December 9, 1978. Altogether, Susan and I now had eight kids. Ironically, Joe was born at 9:09 p.m., and he weighed nine pounds, nine ounces. Moreover, the numbers in his birth date – 12/09/78 – when added together equal ninety-nine. A lot of nines, I have thought many times, and I still wonder if there is some special meaning attached to that fact, though what that may be, I have no idea.

As I have said, Susan and I married on May 8, 1979. Joe, shaking a plastic container of "Dynamints" the entire time, as if providing music for the ceremony, was the only one of our children present as Theresa, the town clerk in Middletown, Connecticut, pronounced us husband and wife during her noon lunch break. Two of her co-workers acted as witnesses. That same day, my divorce from Maribeth became official.

Susan started working in my shop, which, for liability reasons, we kept solely in my name, while the house Sue owned in Portland, Connecticut remained in hers. You might say Joe grew up with the business in his small backpack, where he kept a glasscutter and a few small pieces of glass, which he often used to display his glass-cutting ability when he was as young as age four. Our shop was in a small building attached to another business, a lumberyard.

On December 9, 1983 – Joe's fifth birthday – the lumberyard burned down, along with our shop. As a result, that same day, due to our accountant's quick thinking and help, we bought another building in Colchester. Susan, thinking we could not afford the new space, that it needed too many repairs, was reluctant to proceed with the purchase. I convinced her, however, that after tending to business during the day, I could work on the building at night, and we completed the deal.

Daily, at seven a.m., I would drive sixteen miles from our home in Portland to the shop. Susan would arrive later, at eight, to open its doors for business. She would stay and work until five, when she would return home to feed the kids and do anything else needed around the house. While she was at home with the kids, I would stay at the shop and work until nine, sometimes even later. Then, when I finally returned home, usually between ten and ten-thirty, Sue and I would sit and talk about what had happened at the shop during the day, and what we still needed to buy for the business and the "new" building. I would always pour myself a shot of whiskey on the rocks as we talked, and when Sue went to bed and I stayed up to watch TV, usually I would pour myself another.

At this time, I was forty years old, and now I began drinking every day.

Whenever I wasn't working, I drank, and it began to catch up with me. Change me. Daily, at 2:30 p.m., I would leave whatever job I was working on to go get a drink. By the time Joe was ten or twelve, my drinking had transformed me into an arrogant, ornery man, a stranger to Joe. Though I still loved him, I began picking on him- constantly. Eventually, Susan stopped making supper for us and told Joe that whenever possible, he should just stay out of my way. More and more, I isolated myself from her, Joe, and all our other kids. Drinking had become my way of life. My habit. My addiction. Drinking removed at least some of the edge from my pent-up anger with myself and the world. Finally, I started to realize that I could not, not drink, even though I told Sue I would and should stop. But it was impossible. I had no control of "it." "It" controlled me. Love and a loving family couldn't stop it either. Nothing could. I just wanted to relax. Take the edge off. And have a drink.

I had to do something. And that something was to finally admit what I had despised and shirked from for so long: I needed to ask for help, acknowledge, once and for all, that I couldn't do it alone. That like everyone else in this world, I was not infallible. Far from it. In fact, concerning my drinking, I was powerless. Thus, on November 4, 1994, after drinking daily for the eleven previous years, and now fifty-one years old, I finally did what I had to do to get my life back. Just like when I was lost on Kodiak Island and praying to Him for guidance, so was I lost again now. And just as those Rosary beads of mine were never meant to be tossed away, neither was my life. I needed another "God moment" to save it. As it turned out, all I had to do was ask. And then accept.

PART FOUR
GOD MOMENTS
AND MIRACLES

1.

Wʜᴀᴛ ɪs ᴀ "God moment"? For me, it is when an event occurs not due to coincidence or chance – perhaps, nothing in life is – but one that is due to a divine spirit's intervention for a reason known or unknown to us at the time, but whose meaning becomes clear to us later. In other words, it is something that was either meant, or never meant, to be. That "7" Chase found in the footprint I had left behind while he and another search party were out looking for me? No, he did not just happen to spot it when his gun "accidentally" fell directly on the print. Rather, his gun was meant to fall there to let him and the others know that the print was mine, which direction I was headed, and that I was still alive. Similarly, I needed a "God moment," or a series of such moments, to save my life and my relationship with the people I loved- Sue and our family. By December 1983, our new building – we never would have purchased it if our old building, in another God moment, hadn't burnt down – and its location, coupled with our hard work, enabled our business to prosper. As a result of our success, we were able to hire more employees to help me with the jobs we had contracted and Sue with her office work. We also bought land- forty acres in Colchester, on which we thought we might build and expand our business interests. By 1986, several of our kids were preparing to go off to college. Joe had turned ten, and everything seemed to be going well. Though I was drinking daily, because Sue and I both worked long hours, at least our demanding schedules helped control the amount of alcohol I consumed.

In 1987 – again, I am backtracking here to lead up to the God moment and miracles in my life that occurred in 1994 – two acquaintances of ours approached us concerning some land they were developing, a subdivision that boarded one side of our property. They wanted to know if Sue and I were interested in sharing the cost of constructing a road that would make for easier access to our properties and businesses. In return, they would assume the responsibility of subdividing our land. We agreed to the deal which, as a result, brought phenomenal changes in our life. Soon, we had seven building lots available for sale. The first lot, five acres in size, sold for $110,000. Over the next two years, we sold another for $65,000, and then two more for $60,000 apiece, while selling yet another to pay our share for the road construction and engineering costs. We decided to keep one fifteen-acre lot for ourselves.

With our finances doing so well, Sue and I purchased a cottage in Old Lyme, Connecticut, on the beach at Pointawoods, for $250,000. Along with the cottage, we bought two boats, one that I used every day for recreational enjoyment, and a larger one that I used for deep-sea fishing. Life was indeed good, except for one thing- I had begun drinking a lot. Every day. Though we still owned the house in Portland, now I paid someone to mow the lawn there. That way, I could spend entire summers in Old Lyme to fish and bask in the sun. And drink.

As I have previously stated, it was around this time that I started taking things out on Joe, constantly picking on him and criticizing him. He was our only child still living at home. Our daughter Robin had married, Bob was living with his cousins in East Hampton, Connecticut, and Randy, Ray, and Sara were all away at college. The winter of 1988- '89 saw things worsen even more between Joe and Sue and me as I drank more and more, day and night, while withdrawing further and further into myself, becoming more of a stranger to my family than a devoted husband and father. My life continued its miserable, downward spiral over the next several years, but I didn't seem to mind. After all, wasn't everything still about me and what I wanted? And drinking was one of the things I wanted most, even more than a loving relationship with my family, especially my son Joe.

Along with our cottage in Old Lyme, we also now owned a barn with several horses. Soon, the barn became my refuge from the world, and it was in there, alone, its walls a barrier to all others, all responsibility, all love, that I stole myself away, battened up the hatches to my emotions. And drank.

During the next two years, though our business prospered, Sue and I began to experience financial difficulties. We were in a great deal of debt, and so in the fall of 1991 we decided to sell our cottage in Old Lyme for $235,000. I vividly remember Sue running from the closing, check in hand, once the paperwork was signed and the deal completed so she could go pay off some of our debt. Next, we sold both of our boats, but because Sue loved animals, we bought several sheep and a four-year-old horse named Jillian. Though I was still drinking every day and night, Sue realized that the more work I had to do at home and on our property, the better. The work kept me busy, so, at least during those times, I drank less. As for Joe, now twelve or thirteen, and still our only child living at home, he had plenty of chores to do, but shoveling horse shit wasn't one of them. He vowed never to do it, and he lived up to that promise.

Between 1990 and 2002, all our children, including Joe, were done with school and married. Simultaneously, despite my drinking, our business continued to prosper and, eventually, we owned as many as five horses. I spent countless hours with them, while fixing up the barn until it had the best-looking doors and stalls imaginable. Still, I continued to drink…

Again, I have gotten a bit ahead of myself, so allow me to backtrack to the end of 1993 and early 1994. Because I was drinking heavily, both day and night, while relentlessly abusing Joe, distancing myself from both him and Sue, I finally began to get it through my thick head that I was on my way to ruin. That I was about to lose what mattered most in life- the love of my family. Once and for all I had to swallow my pride and admit to what I had resisted and denied for so long- that I needed help. And that the shame of asking for help was far less than the shame I felt due to my drinking and abusive behavior. Not only was my delusion of infallibility fading, it was now crumbling all around me, and if I failed to change, if I failed to end my drinking, I would be buried beneath the deluge.

One day, toward the end of 1993, I decided to call the alcohol addiction HELP Hotline. I talked with a gentleman for about fifteen minutes, but by the end of our conversation, both he and I concluded I was not an alcoholic. I let Sue know about the call, but she merely listened to what I had to say, while offering nothing in return. We both knew the problem was mine. She could do nothing about it. No one could, except me. So, I continued to drink. After all, I wasn't an alcoholic...Was I? Though I drank heavily, I was also working my tail off to support my family. Alcoholics didn't do that, did they? They couldn't possibly do that...Could they?

Early in September 1994, again sensing that my life was careening toward destruction, that I needed to do something about my drinking – and fast – I decided to call the HELP Hotline again. This time, I was sitting alone in my truck at a job, and I talked with the HELP representative who answered my call for nearly an hour. Still, I failed to acknowledge that I had a problem that I couldn't overcome on my own, because despite all that had happened, and continued to happen, unlike everyone else, I was different. Desperately, I clung to my belief that I was infallible, that I could accomplish what no one else could, that I could do it alone, just as I had on Kodiak Island, thirty years ago...

2.

ON NOVEMBER 3, 1994, I was working at a two-story house Bob, a friend of mine, owned. Bob rented out the upstairs to two women, the downstairs to a young family with two small boys. While working all day on the downstairs windows, I also spent time playing peekaboo in all of them with the kids. Around 4:30, my brother-in-law Ed arrived at the house with the boys' father. Ed wanted me to accompany him to Bob's house in Waterford, Connecticut to have a drink or two. Initially, I declined, Soon, however, what scant ability I had to resist a drink dissipated, and we went to Bob's to enjoy his specialty, a Manhattan, which he served in a big, tall glass, on the rocks.

After finishing the sizeable cocktail, I headed home to Portland via CT Route 9, a forty-mile, four-lane freeway that connects the state's eastern coastline, along with the Lower Connecticut River Valley, to Hartford and the Capital Region. Because I either fell asleep or experienced a blackout – I'm still unsure which – I came to just after missing Exit 7, the exit I was supposed to take, and crashed my truck into the guard rail on the left side of the highway. As a result, I had to call 911 for help so I could get home, along with AAA to come and pick me up. I also called Sue to let her know where I was, but not necessarily the truth about what had happened. Shortly after making my calls, a state trooper arrived, and when I rolled down the window to speak with him, he immediately informed me that, "It smells like a brewery in here."

"I had one drink, no supper, and I keep belching," I explained, of course, omitting the size of the drink.

The trooper then asked me what had happened that caused me to crash into the guard rail. Lying, I replied that a deer had run out in front of me and I had to swerve off the road to avoid hitting him. Meanwhile, a AAA tow truck arrived, and I helped the driver load my truck onto it as the trooper left without ever giving me a ticket.

The accident wasn't the first time I lied about drinking and driving. About a month earlier, as Sue and I left after locking up our shop, she said, "Don't have anything to drink on your way home and we'll have some wine with supper."

"Okay," I agreed. "That sounds good."

As we drove the eighteen miles home to Portland, however, Sue in her car while I drove my truck, I decided to take the slower "scenic" route rather than the highway Sue had taken. Stopping at the first liquor store I came to, I stopped and bought two canned, pre-mixed Manhattans. Then continuing home, as I popped open one can, about to take a swig, thinking of what I had promised Sue, I suddenly asked myself, "Bruce, why did you buy this?" In my heart, I really didn't want to drink. I didn't want to disappoint Sue, and to resist, I quickly tossed both cans out the window.

A mere four miles later, however, spotting another liquor store, submitting to temptation, this time what little willpower I had left tossed out the window, I stopped and bought another two cans. And finished them both before arriving home.

As I entered the house, Sue asked, "What took you so long to get home?"

"I stopped to get gas," I lied, and Sue knew it. She could smell the whiskey on my breath, and a tear slid down her cheek. As I watched the tear fall, I knew no matter what I promised and whom I promised it to, I could not, not pick up a drink. In no way was I its master; I was its slave.

The night after my accident, on November 3, 1994, as I sat on the edge of our bed I said to Sue, "I think I have a problem." As before, she said nothing. There was no need. My lying and drinking were for me to deal with and, finally, I did. The following evening, I attended my first HELP meeting. I went early. Five or six men were already there when I arrived. They greeted me warmly and, after talking awhile, when I asked if I was an alcoholic, no one replied. Later, I asked again. Several times. Until one man answered with a question of his own: "Well, you're here, aren't you?"

Angered by his vague response, I asked, "What do you mean by that? I walk in and I'm captured?"

No one said a thing. Instead, another man went out to his truck and returned with a HELP meeting schedule. Handing it to me he said, "There are twenty questions in here. Take the test when you get home. Answer them as honestly as you can."

Later that night, after arriving home, I took the test, and when I finished and checked my answers, I felt proud that I had gotten seventeen of the twenty questions "right." Until reading further down the answer page, I saw that if you got just three questions "right," you were probably an alcoholic, the same as everyone else who had attended the meeting that night, like Drew. His palsied hands trembling so badly, worse than the shivers I had experienced while lost in the cold on Kodiak Island, I had felt heartbroken for Drew as he read aloud "How It Works" for everyone at the meeting, the "It" in the title meaning the HELP program. Drew had been sober twenty-two years when his wife died. He believed he had gotten sober for her, and now that she was gone, he could resume drinking, which he did for two years. Until at age eighty, he saw the "light" and stopped for good. Not another drop, until age ninety, when his shaking finally ended forever, and he joined his wife in the afterlife.

At the time of my first meeting, I was fifty-one years old, and it had been thirty years since I had wandered out of the woods and, seeking help, knocked on Ron Hurst's cabin door. Back then, and until recently, I had believed I was infallible, that I could defy death. But that night, in front of everyone, a collection of strangers, I acknowledge both to them and myself, "I think I'm an alcoholic, and I need help." As I did, my days of infallibility, of self-delusion, instantly ended. After thirty years, I had finally surrendered and asked for help again. No longer was life and the world, and everything else, all about me, not that it ever had been. It's about us all, everyone and everything, because we all need help. Since that first meeting twenty-six years ago, I have had no desire to drink. Simply miraculous, and not just one "God moment," but more than I can count while realizing who I am and what I am not, and turning everything over to Him, my Higher Power. The path to peace, after years of hardship…

A week after my first meeting, I returned for another. Steve M. was there from the week before, along with a few others, including the man who had greeted me first with a handshake. To this day, in and out of meeting rooms, he continues to struggle to find his path out of alcohol's wilderness.

At my second meeting, I made two new friends. One, John T., was thirteen years sober at the time, while the other, Tall Tom, age twenty-four, had five years of sobriety under his belt. Steve M., John T., and Tall Tom have remained my friends. Occasionally, I still see Steve and Tom, while John and I live near one another in Florida, where I reside during the winter. Along with playing golf together, John and I talk whenever either of us feels troubled. We're always there for each other, either in person or on the phone- the best kind of friendship indeed.

After my second meeting, John and Tom invited me to attend yet another meeting that same week in Marlborough, near Colchester. The late-night meeting was scheduled from 8:30 until 10:00, and it was the longest established meeting in the area where we lived. A man nicknamed "Hardware Stanley," along with his sponsor, had started it, but only after he had been sober for a year. Five years ago, "Hardware" died, after fifty-six years of sobriety during which he had turned his life over to his own Higher Power. It was the only cure for the disease of alcoholism.

Now that I was attending two weekly meetings, John asked me to join him at the late-night one again the following week, and to arrive at 6:30 so we could shoot some pool and eat pizza beforehand. Of course, I agreed, and our friendship and dedication to our HELP Fellowship continued to grow throughout the following summer, as did my enjoyment in living sober. Rejuvenated, as if I had returned from the dead or dying, during a group picnic at Day Pond State Park in Colchester, Tall Tom, twenty-seven years my junior, and I wrestled each other for hours in the park's pond, leaving Tom to wonder aloud, "How is this old bastard keeping up with me?" In retrospect, maybe I should have smiled and told him it was because I was infallible. That I was Superman.

Unlike before, when I had only my horses and a barn to hide myself away from the world, including my wife and the family that I both loved and rejected, I now had a new life. Along with my other two weekly meetings, I also began attending a third- an hour-long, Monday night men's meeting in Portland. Soon, I added a fourth, by attending either a Saturday morning or Saturday night meeting in East Hampton, Connecticut, or a Saturday morning one in nearby Middletown. Along the way, while struggling to establish an honest, open, trusting relationship with my HELP sponsor – that struggle due mostly to the constant interference and objections of my huge male ego, and my reluctance to "just let go" – much to my surprise, I discovered what an *into me see* relationship meant. Despite my ego's silent railings against sharing my life, its dark secrets and shame, with another man, because my sponsor had the courage to share his with me, allowing me to see into him, I finally dropped my guard and did the same. His sponsorship, focusing on the "Twelve Steps" to recovery program and turning my life over to my Higher Power, has changed me forever, as has the Fellowship. The Fellowship primarily means the members of HELP and the gathering of those members in meetings. Sometimes referred to as "The Rooms," Twelve Step meetings are for the people, not the program, and are an integral part of the fellowship of HELP. It brings all us members together and allows us to share our experiences and support one another on the road to recovery. Finally surrendering myself to my Higher Power, along with the Program and its Fellowship, was the beginning of my "learning to live one day at a time, enjoying one moment at a time, while accepting hardship as the path to peace," as the Serenity Prayer encourages us to do. It has saved my life, and the lives of thousands of others.

After attending these weekly meetings for about two years, one evening, as I was about to go out the door, Sue asked, "You're going to a meeting again tonight?" I sensed she wanted me to stay home and spend some time with her, so I paused a few seconds to think about it before replying, "You know, I could be like I used to be."

Knowing neither of us wanted that, Sue gazed at me for several seconds, then merely said, "Oh…" as I continued out the door. There was no way either of us could live with the way "I used to be," because that wasn't living. It was dying, the disease not only killing me, but all that I held dear in my heart. Our marriage. My relationship with Joe and the rest of our kids. Everyone. Everything. There was no going back to the way "I used to be," lost in another kind of wilderness, one perpetually dark, filled with loneliness, disaster, and tears, death its only exit.

3.

One morning, after I had received my three-year sobriety chip, I sat eating breakfast, my back to Sue as she stood at the kitchen counter. As I ate, I heard her say, "Just because you've been sober six months, don't think anything has changed."

Immediately, without missing a beat, I calmly corrected and said, "It's been three years," and nothing more. I was right about that. Time had passed so swiftly, and things had changed. Sue and I were about to embark on a new life together. I had "broken out of the barn," so to speak, learning to enjoy life's moments, sharing them with Sue, no longer selfish, no longer lying, just being me, while falling in love with her again.

Six months after that morning, Sue entered our shop, where I was already at work. Looking me squarely in the eye, happiness twinkling in hers, she smiled and announced, "I just booked a trip for us to the Bahamas."

Smiling as I gazed at her, I replied, "Thank you, God," meaning thank you for everything. For my life and all that had changed in it.

For the joy of living and loving again. For the priceless riches of family and friends. And most of all, I was thanking Him for Sue. Forever humbled, and with an immense gratitude I had never felt before because my ego had blinded me and my drinking had numbed me, I also removed my Rosary from my truck's rearview mirror and placed it in my pants pocket. I have carried it with me ever since. Everyday. Always.

Following our trip to the Bahamas, Sue and I started spending more and more time together. Life wasn't just about business; it was about us, and love. The enjoyment of going places and doing things together. Weekend trips to Boston and New York City. All that we had lost and now shared again. Our love. And time. Precious, precious time. Not a moment to waste, especially considering what lay ahead, just around the corner. Precious, precious time…

On May 5, 2001, I was six years sober when Sue was diagnosed with cancer. Nothing more devastating could have happened to two people so deeply in love. Time and time again, heart shattered, joy and hope suddenly lost, destroyed by fear and sorrow – life's indiscriminate ruthlessness and sheer brutality – I asked God, "Why us?" But for Sue, her diagnosis a death sentence, instantly it became a question of "Why me?" With our remaining time together limited, knowing that I would soon lose Sue forever – at least in this life – I turned to the Fellowship for help. Suddenly, however, I found the message of the Serenity Prayer difficult to accept: "God, grant me the serenity to accept the things I cannot change, courage to change the things I can, and the wisdom to know the difference…" For me, it seemed there was no path to peace. That path, too, had been destroyed by hardship and pain, flooded over by tears, both day and night. Immersed in darkness and depression, more so than at any other time in my life, my grief ate away at my heart. Though I did my best to carry on with our business, often, no sooner would I arrive at a job than, feeling overwhelmed, I would leave. Thank God I had such kind, loyal, loving employees- my nephews Brian and Michael, and my friend Steve. They did their best to help in any way they could. I couldn't have asked for more.

On August 29, 2001, Sue and I closed our business to ease the path to the inevitable and spend as much time together as possible. It was all part of the courage and serenity needed to change what we could – together as one – while accepting that which we could not change, nor could any doctor. Sue's cancer. And death.

To further prepare for that dreaded moment, early in 2002, we sold our farm and horses and bought a house on East Main Street in Portland, where we would live together until that moment arrived, and then I would live alone. Sue spent many of her remaining days working on the house so that, other than general maintenance, I would have little to do regarding upkeep and repairs. If not for my sponsor David's help, along with that of the Fellowship and a host of other friends, with doomsday rapidly approaching, I think I would have gone insane. I knew I could not, in desperation, return to the bottle to numb my fear and pain. There would have been too much shame and failure in that, along with a rejection of all that had changed in my life. A rejection of both God and my sober self. My true self. I had to continue to honor my commitment to Sue, my family, the Fellowship, and the Program that had rescued me from the disease and slow suicide. All that I had ever asked for in the Serenity Prayer. All that we can ever ask for in learning how to live.

On January 3, 2003, after spending twenty-two months as her primary caretaker, Sue passed away. Though at that moment and I felt more lost and alone than ever before, just like on Kodiak Island, the God of my understanding was always with me, as He is with me today, and will be forever. I have lived a life far beyond my wildest dreams, a rollercoaster of a life, but one filled with love and abundance, for which I can only be grateful. God has a plan, and though I know not where His plan will take me, I know my children and grandchildren love me, and so does Sue in Heaven. What more can I ask for? What more could I, or anyone else, possibly want?

Final Thoughts

As a young man, despite my ignorance and selfishness – my belief that everything was about me, and I was infallible – I tried my best to bring to life's "game" as many of the lessons I had learned as possible. They were the lessons, rooted in Christian beliefs and morality my parents had taught me, those based on a respect for all God's creatures and creations, and on the principle of treating others as I would have them treat me. My parents were Catholic, and they raised me as such, doing their best to instill in me those Christian tenets that would make me a good man and the world a better place. Again, though I have failed at times, I believe I have tried my best to live up to those principles and learn from my mistakes, which is the most any of can do in trying to learn how to live.

I have always believed in a Higher Power and, as a young man lost on Kodiak Island, all that I had been taught, all that I believed, and all I had succeeded or failed at, had been exactly what was needed for me to survive that experience. In other words, everything was as it should have been and was supposed to be, just as it is today. As I have said, though we all get lost at times and feel overwhelmed by the events in our lives – Why me? Why us? – I believe God has a plan, no matter how unfair, how cruel and incomprehensible that plan may seem at times. Somehow, someway, perhaps in another lifetime, we will discover its meaning and make sense of it. We must maintain an open mind in that regard, or wander through life lost and afraid, no light, map, or compass to guide us through life's perils, or even its good times. After all, we learn and grow from both the "good" and the "bad," and how we handle both.

After my experience on Kodiak Island, the beliefs that my parents had instilled in me carried me through the next thirty years of my life, but with little spiritual growth. Until age fifty-one, by which time, drinking heavily day and night, I lost my way again, this time in alcohol, a far more lonely, deadly struggle than the one I had experienced on Kodiak Island, where I never panicked, never thought about dying. But with my soul all but bankrupt, I was dying now, and so were my relationships with the people I loved, my wife Sue and our children, with all that remained of my sick, crumbling heart. "Use it, or lose it," as the saying goes, and I was on the brink of losing everything. Drinking was killing it all, and it was murdering me. I needed a "God moment" to save my life, and on November 4, 1994 that moment arrived. I attended my first HELP meeting, admitted to myself and a group of strangers that I couldn't stop drinking on my own, and that I needed help because I was an alcoholic.

As with everything else that had occurred in my life, that God moment was meant to happen, and I was meant to go through hell until it did. Now about to turn seventy-seven, I have not had a drink since, nor have I ever desired one. Loneliness and despair had become my teachers, and there were no substitutes, until the Program and the Fellowship came along, and I learned to live again. It was alright to ask for help, and it was alright to accept it. It was what I needed to do to free my soul from the dumpster I had created of my life, along with the Rosary that hung from its door, those beads now and forever tucked safely away in my own pocket full of miracles. I will have them with me when I see Sue again.

Since that first HELP meeting, I have come to see my spiritual growth as a continual process, one without end, not even when I die. The HELP Program and Fellowship tell us to find our own power greater than ourselves, our own concept of God. Whatever works for you. That search for a Higher Power is the start of *willingness*, and that was what it took for this alcoholic, Joseph Bruce LaChance, to get started on the path to recovery. Adhering to that path, rather than wandering lost, desperate and alone, allows me to both give and accept love. It is all good and, as we say in the Fellowship, it all comes down to three commitments: Trust God. Clean House. Help Others.

For me, those three commitments represent the meaning of Life itself. They tell me to live the best I can today by turning my life over to my Higher Power, keeping the focus on me through continual self-assessment, and accepting all that I cannot change, including all that my children and grandchildren are and what they do. I can only find my own business, and mind it. And equally important: be available, as I finally learned to do with the woman I loved, and still love, with all my heart; contribute when asked; and always remember that unsolicited advice is no more than criticism, which may hurt and rile me, but with God's help, I will soothe myself by refusing to act likewise. Instead, I will be kind, both to myself and others, and embrace them as God does, especially Sue, when we see each other again, hold hands, and take a walk together in Heaven, and maybe on Kodiak Island, too.

About the Book

IN **1964,** WHILE serving as a radioman in the United States Navy on Kodiak Island, Alaska, twenty-one-year-old Joseph Bruce LaChance set out to hunt one of nature's most fearsome creatures- a giant Kodiak brown bear. Expecting to return to the naval base after a three-day expedition, instead LaChance suddenly found himself lost in the wilderness for ten days without a compass, map, or any other means of guidance, while running out of food. With his chances for survival near zero, LaChance had only his undaunting perseverance and faith, both in himself and God, to overcome death's odds. His struggle to survive, however, did not end on Kodiak Island. Thirty years later, he would face another life or death struggle while again lost and alone, but in a different kind of wilderness- alcoholism. LaChance's miraculous story provides a profound lesson for us all, not only in how to survive, but to live our lives with love and dignity, at peace with both ourselves and what we conceive as our own Higher Power.

ABOUT THE AUTHOR

NOW SEVENTY-SEVEN YEARS old, Bruce LaChance divides his time between his summer home in Maine and his winter residence in Florida. Clean and sober since 1994, Mr. LaChance remains forever grateful to the HELP Program and Fellowship, as well as family and friends, for his ability to live, love, and enjoy life one day at a time. Self-diagnosed with dyslexia, he enlisted the help of friend and novelist Michael A. Milardo to write his story.

CPSIA information can be obtained
at www.ICGtesting.com
Printed in the USA
LVHW030800211122
733624LV00009B/886